Studies in the Anthropology of North American Indians

Editors: Raymond J. DeMallie and Douglas R. Parks

The Medicine Men

Oglala Sioux Ceremony and Healing

Thomas H. Lewis

Published by the

University of Nebraska Press, Lincoln & London

in cooperation with

the American Indian Studies Research Institute,

Indiana University

Library of Congress Cataloging
in Publication Data
Lewis, Thomas H.
The medicine men: Oglala Sioux
ceremony and healing /
Thomas H. Lewis.
P.   cm. – (Studies in the anthropol-
ogy of North American Indians)
Includes bibliographical references.
ISBN 0-8032-2890-2 (alk. paper)
ISBN 0-8032-7939-6 (pbk.)
1. Oglala Indians – Medicine.
2. Oglala Indians – Rites and cere-
monies. 3. Sun-dance. 4. Folk
medicine – South Dakota. 5. Pine
Ridge Indian Reservation (S.D.) –
Social Life and customs. I. Title.
II. Series.
E99.O3L49   1990
615.8'8208997509783 – dc20
89-22508   CIP

First Bison Book printing: 1992
Most recent printing indicated
by the last digit below:
10 9 8 7 6 5 4 3

Acknowledgments
of previously published material
appear on pages 11–12.

To my field companions, Linda and David

Contents

Introduction

This book describes some of the men who practice the indigenous healing arts of the Oglala Sioux. They provide advisory and therapeutic services to the rural population of some twelve thousand residents of the Pine Ridge Reservation in South Dakota. I will examine techniques, personal histories and qualities, problems addressed, patients, and results, and will attempt to describe past as well as present practices, linking observable patterns to underlying structures.

The Oglala people are the westernmost division of the Tetons, one of the three major groups of the Dakotas, or Sioux, and identify themselves as *Lak'ota*. They occupy the arid grasslands of Pine Ridge Reservation, a vast landscape with a few small towns and infrequent isolated cabins. The Oglalas once roamed a much wider universe, the valleys of the Platte and Missouri, Yellowstone, Powder, and Bighorn, where lie the sites of partly remembered battles with neighboring tribes in early historic times and of the later wars with the whites that brought an end to their nomadic way of life and forced profound changes in their culture.

Along with the destruction of the buffalo herds that constituted their essential commissary the Sioux suffered heavy and repeated military defeats. They were deprived of weapons, transport, and accustomed means of livelihood, and were sequestered on reservations. Hunting became unproductive, rations were meager. Administrators made an effort to integrate their charges into the rapidly enveloping white life patterns with but little success. The Sioux continued to live, and many do still, in small scattered communities composed of extended families or combinations that resemble the old hunting group, the *t'iyospaye*. Today's medicine men practice within these social groupings.

The Sioux came into history with the reputation of being dominating, arrogant, volatile, and dangerous. This was, of course, not an objective characterization, but possibly accurate. Nomadic, wide-ranging, and truculent, they were feared by their enemies and were a military model for their allies. With stunning suddenness they were reduced in number and transformed into passive wards of a distant government. They were increasingly dependent, increasingly suppressed, increasingly impoverished.

Children were extracted from families and placed in schools which resembled disciplinary barracks. The adults had passing and disheartening experiences with farming and ranching and lasting experience with demoralizing idleness. The land was lost, most of it, and loss of effective control of the remainder followed. A cascade of short-term programs were proposed to encourage adaptation to the cataclysmic alterations in almost everything the Lakota culture had developed.

Many Christian proselytizing sects flooded onto the reservations, competing with each other to save souls. Some denominations stayed and grew. Others receded, their buildings abandoned to other enthusiasts, or boarded up, vandalized, or burned. In recent decades there have been attempts to intertwine aboriginal motifs into Christian liturgies and architecture. One group created a church of glass and beams in tipi style with a "central fire" altar which on completion resembled a novelty cafe. Another denomination decorated its chapel with shields, arrows, and pipes, a peculiar blending of the themes of war and peace.

More aesthetically pleasing than these abortive syncretisms were the autochthonous revivals that grew into the Ghost Dance, Native American Church, Sioux Religion, pan-Indianism, and the Red Power movement. The Sun Dance was revived. It had been proscribed in earliest reservation years as reactionary, distracting, distastefully savage, and potentially or politically dangerous. It was brought back cautiously in 1930 or earlier, sometimes as a part of "Indian celebrations," later in more nearly traditional form. Secular dancing was adapted into Wild West performances and became show business or, nearer home, prize competitions and the recreations of the powwow. After a century of such mutations and erasures, large parts of the aboriginal culture remained. Some changed, but little was extinguished. Least altered, as we shall come to appreciate, were the healers and their ritual procedures.

Treaties with the Plains tribes had stipulated that medical services would be provided to the reservations. White physicians and medical teams found that indigenous physicians were still at work and competitive. In keeping with the times, attempts were immediately set on foot to eradicate them. After all, a national effort had long been devoted to the suppression of frauds and charlatans, patent-medicine salesmen, "yarb" doctors, and the like. Suppression of the medicine men was a logical extension of the national cleansing, and was consistent with the thought that civilization and education of federal wards entailed a homogenization of belief and practice.

But aboriginal conservatism triumphed. The condemnation of the older healing sects did not bring an acceptance of the new. Today the medicine men continue with a system that is parallel to Western medicine, interacting with it minimally or not at all, and preserving in the process many of the cultural antiquities of the Sioux.

The Sioux Nation today considers itself a sovereign political unit, still in contention with the United States government over autonomy and territory. "We own everything from the Great Lakes to Denver. We want it all back, including the Black Hills," is a refrain repeated at political rallies to laughter and applause. Within the Nation, the Oglalas are distinct from the other Sioux groups. The processes of accommodation to and assimilation with the engulfing white society were never completed. Many features of white American culture were never even minimally accepted by the Sioux. A disconcerting level of mutual hostility and mutual discrimination between white and Indian still exists, played out painfully and especially in economic and judicial arenas. Moreover, intratribal conflicts between "progressive" and "traditional" Oglala factions often prevent united and constructive action. When the social analyst looks at Oglala life a century after the end of military conflict with the United States Army, the striking dynamic is the retention and renewal of much of the traditional Oglala world-view, religion, hunting-group social organization, ceremonial structures, and practices of healing. The Oglalas, while living precariously in the present, cling to the memory and practice of ancestral life and transpose treasured fragments of those memories and ways into new contexts. What remains of the old culture is often of immeasurable value to the participant Oglalas and to the attentive non-Teton observer.

The Development of a Method and Point of View

Why study the Sioux? They have already occupied many ethnographers, historians, and educators of discernment and scholarship. Much has been written and more is being written without yet reaching a sufficiency. Political and economic issues run so deep that civil servants, politicians, opportunists, and activists may never lack for material. Urgent human needs and vivid human processes on the several Sioux reservations attract students of varied persuasions. I am one of these, and what I was able to learn was so much a function of my own personal mode of inquiry that the reader may ask how my point of view developed and what methods came to be used.

I grew up among the enemies of the Sioux. The people of southern Montana had fought them in living memory. They considered the Sioux supremely dangerous and only dubiously contained. From these Montanans I acquired a baggage of ideas and stories later to be considerably revised and rebalanced. My grandparents ran cattle and horses. An uncle trailed stock south to the Lodge Grass and lived on Crow Reservation economy, where beef quarters were the common coinage. Another uncle grew wheat on leased Crow ranges. A neighbor knew Curley, the

4

Crow scout, and the men on the burial detail after the Custer fight. His description of the general as "an abusive son of a bitch" came from a soldier's and working man's point of view that I've never heard elsewhere. Liver-Eating Johnson, scourge of the Sioux, was sheriff of our town. My grandmother told stories of parties of Cheyennes camping in the summer on the creek below our house, drying meat and leaving burials in the trees. Crow children went to the Rocky Flats school with my mother. Cousins went to school with Crow kids at Pryor, where "anything they could take away from us got thrown down the privy."

All of this was storied about. It transported childhood imaginations to the great old days of fighting, an imagination that was further shaped, colored, and highlighted by Charles Russell, who spoke for us then and belonged deeply to our romantic souls. Tales of raids and forts on hilltops and last stands in the timber had no abstract quality for us. We could look out the kitchen window to landscapes where any of those stories might have been acted out, to hilltops and buttes where arrow points and bits of harness testified to stories we had not yet heard.

Still, we didn't need to rely on memories or imaginations because actual Indian families came along the benches on horseback and in spring wagons. They were there all summer, doing odd jobs, trading horses, or competing in the rodeos. We knew the ones our age, and we knew the old folks. We knew with a very lively sense that the country had almost-yesterday been abandoned by Gros Ventres, Sioux, and Blackfeet, the "finest light cavalry the world has ever known." While looking for stock we saw the tipi rings on Elbow Creek and the pictographs by the river at Joliet. There were still scatters of beads on the hillsides, hammerstones and flint points in the fields, and we never quite finished with impressions and half-understandings.

My mother encouraged both curiosity and imagination. My father was a gregarious man with a Welsh respect for eloquence and oral tradition. After he and I agreed I was grown up, about age five, his idea of an education for me was to introduce me to people he thought were powerful or interesting. I was taken to shake hands with peculiar travelers in blue turbans, circus owners, virtuosos, boxing champions, authors, surgeons, and performers. His father and my uncles had participated in the unionization wars in Glamorganshire and in the American West. They had an affinity, so to speak, with other tribal people, an identity of old battles and individual assertions. With them I spent many hot afternoons in canvas lodges on the Greasy Grass and at Browning. Who were those grave handshakers, those Indian police and medicine men of great presence, ominous to me in their mysteriousness? I didn't know then, and they left another residue of unanswered questions.

University gave me a lasting love for descriptive study. After graduating in medicine, I practiced in rural New Mexico. Learning the botany of the highlands and coasts of western Mexico brought repeated encounters with Apaches, Tarahumaras, Huicholes, Coras, Yaquis, and Seris. A scientific focus succeeded observation when another physician, a botanist, and I designed two month-long trips to the Huichole villages in the mountains of Nayarit to get background on the original peyote users. The drug was then of interest to psychiatry because its effects resembled (slightly) the ideopathic ("spontaneous") psychoses. We found Mexican ranchers who introduced us to the *cantadores* and *curanderos* in the remote barrancas, and there we lived and half-starved while filling notebooks and plant presses. The story of the ritual use of peyote has been well told by later travelers, on the basis of the fine old classics of Karl S. Lumholtz and Bernardino de Sahagún.[1]

I trained in psychiatry and psychoanalysis during the period when interest in personality dynamics was at full flower in university programs. Careful listening and an honest respect for the experiences of patients was the emphasis, an approach that guided me to a research year at the National Institute for Mental Health and a continuing relationship with the Psychiatric Branch of the Office of Naval Research. A project in 1963 led to the Türüyo of the Palaomeu and Tapanahoni rivers in Surinam to conduct cognitive studies of a nonacculturated, forest-dwelling, hunting tribe. We paid special attention to the curers and shamans. Our Rorschach protocols gave us a great volume of data, a few medical and psychiatric papers, and lasting friendships "in the bush."

During these years the Washington Psychoanalytic Institute gave me a deep immersion in the analytic experience. The participant observation of Harry Stack Sullivan was a strong influence on many clinicians, and interdisciplinary studies were popular. Erik Erikson wrote on childhood development and society; Francis Hsu on psychological anthropology; Werner Muensterberger initiated a series The Psychoanalytic Study of Society; Oscar Lewis produced detailed biographies of Mexican and Puerto Rican families; and Robert Coles produced his series on the experiences of children in disadvantaged and minority groups. All seemed to offer, in their different ways, valuable understanding of aspects of Sioux social problems. In retrospect, it seems to me that the disciplines then were open to and hopeful of something like a unified field of sociology, psychiatry, and anthropology. The walls of parochialism have grown higher since.

Approach and Method in Medical Anthropology

It was with this background that I encountered the Sioux. With other companions and with other destinations in mind, we stopped at a small Pine Ridge café in 1965. Sioux music was on the juke box. Coffee was ten cents an hour. Friendly people, several of them, urged that we visit the Sun Dance, the Tribal Council offices, and Holy Rosary Mission. All were pleasantly hospitable. The open friendliness had in it some promotion of the local sights, but, more engagingly, was a genuine and sustained effort to make Teton life interesting to visitors. This Lakota attitude was to change profoundly in less than a decade. My notes cover the time of that transformation.

We returned at Sun Dance time in 1967 with notebooks and camera and a letter of invitation from the tribal council, intending to observe unobtrusively the public parts of the ceremony, to make round-the-clock notes on the Sun Dance, and to seek out interviews with indigenous medical practitioners. I had my children with me. We borrowed horses, ate at the community kitchen, sat in the shade of the lodges in the heat of the day, never missed a moment of the ceremony or a minute of the dancing, and tried to get a few naps between midnight and dawn despite the never-ending drums.

My approach to the healers was uncomplicated and collegial: "I am a physician. Tell me how you approach medical problems." The response was gratifying, and far more than I had anticipated. From the beginning, I was expected to participate, to visit distant homes, to help with locating singers and equipment, to accompany the medicinal-plant collectors. The Mental Health Service and the U.S. Public Health Hospital were similarly welcoming. I learned much there from staff meetings and outreach visits with Social Services personnel, from psychiatrist Dr. Carl Mendell, anthropologist Eileen Maynard, and from the hospital administrators, tribal liaison officers, tribal police, and legal services. The staff at Holy Rosary Mission School was vigorously interested in educational reform. "These kids don't want to be Indians; they want to be cowboys," said one of the Jesuit fathers. "They come here bright and curious, from families that have incomes of three hundred dollars a year. By the time they are in the sixth grade they see they are not going to make it on their terms in a white economy that wants day laborers, so they drop out. It's a rare one who makes it to high school."

The following year (1968), I was privileged to work in August as a physician at the Mental Health Clinic and, for a time thereafter, as a psychiatric consultant. The experience was illuminating and opened many doors in the Public Health Service, Bureau of Indian Affairs, the Sioux Sanatorium for Tuberculosis, and the Veterans' Administration Hospital in Hot Springs, key elements in the medical services of which the Pine Ridge people were clients. From 1969 through 1972, while maintaining these contacts, I gave greater time to working with Oglala practitioners and their patients and to completing notes on what seemed to make the indigenous medical services operate. Residence with Sioux families allowed extended observation of the meaning of rituals and the recording of notes on myth and ceremony. Many good friends and indefatigable helpers of those days are now gone from life or have passed to different activities. I hope they approve, or would have approved, of my organization on these pages of what they told me and showed me.

I am particularly grateful to Peter Catches, Robert Holy Dance, and Frank Fools Crow, who fell easily into a teaching mode of physician-to-physician. They became my friends as well as collaborators. I have followed their wishes, expressed to me and explicitly repeated during my studies at Pine Ridge, to record the healing arts they practice so that knowledge and understanding of them might be disseminated. They had found, especially from the new Mental Health Clinic, a friendly interest in indigenous medical practices and were of a mind to share the knowledge they valued with others who would equally respect it. The path had been prepared for me without my knowing it, and for this I must recognize the effective and humane work of the psychiatrists who preceded me at the Public Health Hospital. They established a tradition of "new and powerful and trustworthy medicine men."

In 1988 I revisited my mentors to be sure of explicit permission to use their names and quotations. One demurred, saying that he now espoused bitter anti-white philosophies and had developed a fundamentalist purification of his ritual. Because of his insistence that he currently rejects all elements of what he formerly taught, he appears in these pages anonymously.

I am likewise indebted to Paul Stuart of the Mental Health Unit, Public Health Hospital, Pine Ridge; to Stephen Feraca, Bureau of Indian Affairs, Washington, D.C.; and to Brice Lay, Superintendent of the Bureau of Indian Affairs at Pine Ridge. Helpful over many years were Delpha Watters, Orville and Lavon Schwarting, Howard Blue Bird, Stephen Gay, Joe White Face, Francis Coutier, Good Voice Elk, Paul Apple, William Horn Cloud, Edgar Red Cloud, Amos Lone Hill, Kermit Bear Shield, Plenty Wolf, and William Schweigman. Raymond Bucko, S.J., helped with the identification of Lakota plant names in Chapter 6 by checking them with knowledgeable Oglalas. Kay Young assisted with portions of the ethnobotanical material. The drawings are by Gwen Leighton.

Between 1974 and 1979 I taught medical anthropology at

Georgetown University School of Medicine, Washington, D.C., and am indebted to my students for a richer perspective on indigenous healers. Raymond J. DeMallie exhaustively reviewed the several versions of the manuscript and systematized the transcription of Lakota words, following the orthography of Eugene Buechel, S.J., *Lakota-English Dictionary* (1970). Since most Lakota words are accented on the second syllable, stress is not marked there. However, some words are accented on the first syllable, and in these cases stress is indicated by an accent mark.

The core manuscript was completed in 1972. The intense politicization of Pine Ridge thereafter made further field work difficult, even dangerous. Rural people were confronted by powerful activist and conservative factions in an atmosphere of growing lawlessness. They had to declare allegiances for immediate safety and to live year round with their decisions. Older friendships often had to be put in moratorium when racism and violence flourished in a destructive political climate. In 1972 Wounded Knee was occupied by confrontational mobs, some of whom were Oglalas, some not. Gordon, Nebraska, was occupied by federal forces in reaction. A perimeter of armored vehicles was thrown up around Wounded Knee "to contain the insurrection." Ammunition was expended and people were killed. The barricades immobilized the "Federals" and were a sieve for the "Indians." Buildings were trashed and fired, leasing ranchers were driven out, hatreds were established which are still nourished. A flood of journalism fed the national appetite for sensational accounts of the "Second Battle of Wounded Knee." Much of the flood was shallow and distorted, slanted, partisan, and wildly inaccurate. In the spate, the thought of presenting material from a quieter time appeared irrelevant or outdated.

In the decade after Wounded Knee II, when civil strife sought and found fresh tinder in other parts of the nation, some measure of quiet returned to Pine Ridge. Time was found to assess what had been destroyed and what had been gained from the uproar. The victims are better judges of that than the protagonists, and we have not heard much from them yet. The silence after Wounded Knee II was followed by the appearance of a new group of well-studied, well-presented publications about the Oglalas. These encouraged me to reconsider my notes in the light of this wider and deeper appreciation of Lakota culture.

This is not a psychological or psychoanalytic study. It was not motivated by diagnostic preconceptions. No plans for future action or recommendations for change are offered, nor were any ever intended. The Sioux have been inundated with evaluations, sociological analyses, and ingenious humanitarian recommendations since the very beginning of their reservation life. Those efforts have had minimal operational value and for the most part have subsided into obscurity. Instead of contributing to this futile mass I have tried instead to present my observations on the human phenomena that interested me, to be as objective as possible, and to explain what I think I have understood. I had no prearranged formulations to support, represented no agency or institution, and espoused no faction. In the churning atmosphere of social conflict and change; economic agonies; political, governmental, and educational crosscurrents; and the small-town contentiousness of reservation life, the outsider finds no safety in neutrality or in ingratiating flexibility. I chose to follow neither one nor the other. I recorded the material as it was observed, and the interpretations are my own. I am aware that other observers may well emphasize elements of which I was unaware, that anyone's personal impressions cannot be identical with the impressions of another participant, and that a practiced ceremonialist will point to gaps in my appreciation and comprehension. These are unavoidable. Much depended on the understandings and the candor of my Oglala companions in the inquiry. I doubt that many of them will read these pages. Participants generally have slight interest in the productions of note takers other than being quoted correctly. Other readers are advised to approach these pages in the way they were written, as leaves from a notebook. The years I speak about are gone. So are many of the people.

Some of the material in this book has appeared in different form in professional journals. Notes on the Sun Dance were published in the *Pine Ridge Research Bulletin* (1968) and the *Plains Anthro-*

pologist (1972); on the Catch-the-Stone ceremony in *Hospital and Community Psychiatry* (1974); on *cʿaŋli icahiye* in the *Plains Anthropologist* (1980); on *heyokʿa* in the *Pine Ridge Research Bulletin* (1970), *Anthropos* (1974), the *Journal of Operational Psychiatry* (1981), and the *Plains Anthropologist* (1982); on depression and mutism in the *American Journal of Psychiatry* (1975); on Holy Dance's illness in the *Annals of Internal Medicine* (1980); on shamanic medicine in the *Journal of Group Psychotherapy, Psychodrama, and Sociometry* (1982) and the *Plains Anthropologist* (1980). "The Contemporary *Yuwipi*" appeared in *Sioux Indian Religion,* edited by Raymond J. DeMallie and Douglas R. Parks (University of Oklahoma Press, 1987), © University of Oklahoma Press, 1987. It is used with the permission of the publisher.

1. Getting Acquainted: Pine Ridge, 1967

Highway 18 crosses the Missouri River at Fort Randall and finds for the first time a western landscape, more western through Bonesteel, Winner, Mission, Vetal, Martin, Swet, through the Rosebud Reservation and the green expanses of Bennett County. Remember those towns—when you tire of rougher life you will need to come back for a good dinner and a motel bed, and maybe a drink from a behind-the-counter bottle, shaped like a naked girl and labeled "The Old Man's Private Stuff." There are no comforts like these west of Batesland, where the Pine Ridge boundary runs north and south. It angles eventually to encompass 2,780,000 acres, all grassland conspicuously more arid than the surrounding cultivated country. The reservation is dotted with diminutive, widely separated communities, some with no more than a one-room store, an undependable gas pump, a few wooden houses, a tent.

This is "Indian country"—Manderson, Potato Creek, Kyle, Oglala, Number 4, Red Shirt Table, Wanblee. The landscape is monotonous, featureless, and empty to some eyes; to others it is appealing for its clean simplicity. In midsummer the undulating prairie is covered with dry yellow grasses and a glinting yellow haze. To the far south a line of low hills marks the Nebraska border. Almost to the horizon, a rough speck marks an unused dance bowery standing in absolute solitude. Another mote further on becomes, through field glasses, the weathered houses of Wolf Creek. A narrow road to the north leads to distant

Wounded Knee. The highway, after a long time, reaches the town of Pine Ridge, largest on the reservation, an irregular sprawl of faded wood and tar paper in tuneless contrast to the federal compound of green lawns and cantonment-like buildings. In the native quarters of the town, so to say, because the newcomer's impression is of a colonial outpost, the dooryards are treeless, grassless, eroded dirt. The streets are unpaved. Some of the dusty views have a sameness with the poverty hamlets of the Deep South.

Arriving from the east, the highway passes a track to the Sun Dance grounds, winding down to ford the creek and branching to the rodeo corrals and carnival. The hill above, in season, is thick with tents, cooking fires, aged automobiles, a few tipis. The road is ground into fine, ankle-deep dust. Groups of boys on horseback race along the heated ruts, yelling and laughing.

The highway into town passes slapped-together soft drink and hamburger stands with faintly lettered cardboard signs: "Navajo tacos, fry bread, steamburgers, pop." Next, the moccasin factory (closed), the fishhook-snelling factory (boarded up), a boarded-up church. On the right are a piece of broken sidewalk, abandoned store fronts, a gas station, a dirt side road to Velma's Cafe and Motel (closed), and a battered bit of stone wall where the old fellows with canes come to idle and gossip. On the left are the new post office and the massive Billy Mills Community Center in the United States Postal Service architectural style. The cavernous empty basement has only blowing piles of wastepaper. The upper floor is a gymnasium fitted out for basketball and used for powwows in cold weather. Up the street is a modern shopping center. It was a tribal building enterprise and when completed was leased, nearly at a loss, to a white off-reservation merchandizing-management corporation. It offers a suburban-standardized food market and clothing, at monopoly prices, and is a welcome bit of home to tourists.

The southwestern quadrant of town is laid out with rows of well-kept, spacious, nearly identical white houses, subsidized quarters for Bureau of Indian Affairs and other federal employees. The lawns are clipped, the trees stately, and the yards securely fenced. Across the road are the offices of the BIA, OEO (Office of Economic Opportunity), residential school, Tribal Council. Beyond is the jail and Law and Order. Near the highway where it turns north in the center of town are the federally financed housing project and the federally funded nursing home. On the hilltop, with gracefully curving entrance roads, is the Public Health Hospital. On the slope, behind and out of sight for privacy or from embarrassment, are the family homes for hospital workers. The compound is a new housing development out of American suburbia—sprinklers and flowers, basements and garages, paved streets and walks, fresh paint, and a stout barbed-wire perimeter. It is as remote from the realities of the reservation as placement and design can make it. Beyond the fence is open range.

The highway, running north now, dips into a shallow coulee and passes the age-softened buildings of Holy Rosary Mission. Here are a mission school, quiet walks, gardens, old trees. The grave of Red Cloud is on a sun-hammered nearby slope amid the drying summer weeds—"the first man to win a war with the United States." Farther on are Oglala, Payabya, a marker about the sporadic fighting after Wounded Knee, a memorial to *T'a-śuŋkak'okip'api*, "Old-man-they-fear-even-his-horses," and the townlet of Calico. Shortly beyond are the western boundary of the reservation; Oelrichs, South Dakota; and the Wyoming country.

Go back to Pine Ridge and follow the road south. One step across the state line is Whiteclay, which began as a whiskey ranch, serving legal Nebraska alcohol to thirsty reservation customers. It was notorious for violence a hundred years ago and still is today. The town is constructed of bars. Several are alleged to accept willingly ADC (Aid to Dependent Children) checks. Newcomers are warned seriously to avoid all of the bars, and the Jumping Eagle Inn especially. Arguments and knifings are said to be routine among Indian patrons, and certain if one is a hated white. The bartender denied the reputation (I had to inquire, at least), sold us good beer and conversation, and made us believe the Jumping Eagle was the safest purveyor of moist goods this side of Denver. He was right that afternoon, but he hinted that Stabler's across the street was, maybe, hazardous. On other days, the insensate bodies one can see on the street in the mid-summer sun or on porches and in alleyways on cold days are not corpses, but the swollen purple faces on some seemed nearly past resuscitation.

Randy's market in Whiteclay is an old-time jammed-and-cluttered general store. The high false front is lettered "Šina — Tiyobleca — Canwaken — Lakota Masopiye" *(Šina — Tʻiyobleca — Cʻáŋwakʻiŋ — Lakʻota Mazopʻiye),* "Blankets — Tents—Saddles—Sioux Store." The convivial clerks know every reservation inhabitant, old and new. "How's come you *offer* to cash out-of-state personal checks before I ask? I've never been in here before!" "Oh, we knew you were coming. To the hospital, right? Everybody knows. Moccasin telegraph." Groceries, farm clothes, boots and Stetsons, beads, dentalium shells, hair pipes, feathers, finished beadwork of Oglala women, Sioux fashions in dresses, shawls, and finery.

Halfway back to Pine Ridge from Whiteclay is the Three Moccasin public campground. Quiet and beautiful, it was a tribal investment that began with well-appointed campsites encircling a huge oval of tended meadow, with running water, hot showers, and a resident ranger. Planned for the income tourists might bring and large enough for community gatherings, it was within two years trashed into oblivion, covered in empty bottles and beer cans. "It's our reservation and we can do anything we want with it. We'll pave the sonafabitch with paper plates and shitty diapers. How you like that for aboriginal conservation?"

While you are thinking of an answer, let's ride back to city center and begin to meet people and look around. The Crazy Horse Cafe is small, cinder block, once painted white, surrounded by blowing dust. Horses droop in the heat along the front window. Cars scatter irregularly about the dirt lot. A screen door keeps the flies in. A counter and a half-dozen tables, no two alike, are served indifferently by several angry-looking young women. Perhaps they are serving out jail time—no other explanation presents itself to account for those faces—and who would

dare to ask? The menu is simple: hamburgers, cheese sandwiches, soda pop, coffee. The customers know there is no other
café closer than Rushville, some twenty-five miles away in Nebraska. They use a blend of patient waiting, insistence, and glum
acceptance to get something to eat despite the sullen resistance.
The café is a tribal business. Its open hours are brief and uncertain. Yet it pays, in the reservation waiting game, to keep an eye
on the Crazy Horse. When it's open it can be a flowing spring of
news and gossip. Its patrons are there for talk. The juke box is
loaded with "Sioux favorites," drum and song-and-dance spe-
cialties labeled "Canyon Records, Phoenix"—round dances,
rabbit dances, grass dances—and there is no better place anywhere for learning to distinguish them. If you are looking for
someone, he might come in. If you have nothing else to do,
someone will surely know about jobs or a rodeo schedule, a "49"
(round dance) or a powwow.

Law and Order

The police force is called "Law and Order" and a tribal police-
man is "Law and Order" by ordinary address. When one considers the size of the reservation, the large numbers of arrests for
disorderly behavior and drunkenness, the ever-confusing matters
of jurisdiction with state police, county police, and federal mar-
shals, Law and Order's lot cannot be a happy one. Over time, by
doing psychiatric consultations at the jail and emergency room, I
came to know many Law and Order officers. I had a potential of
usefulness to them and I was not likely a problem, but I did know
that these were not the only reasons for their consistently friendly
courtesies. For information and transmitting messages I was repeatedly grateful. One midnight, in black darkness, I tried to
leave the Sun Dance grounds by driving behind the tents, and put
a wheel in a deep hole. Law and Order brought up a van full of
the freshly arrested and had the car lifted bodily onto level
ground.

We sat around the Law and Order office one afternoon, waiting for a conference on delinquents and talking with Coats Blue

Horse. Two Bulls said, "I cuss this job every day but I can't stay away on vacations. I've stayed with it for years and always think about quitting."

One investigator talked of the glue sniffers, the angry adolescents, and the conspicuously psychiatric cases who still have to be handled by the police:

> We've got Myrtle ———— in jail right now. She's sick and she's wild. She's a lot like Lizzy ———— in 1963. She was on some kind of psychiatry pills and got crazy on them. She carried a rifle. I searched up and down this here creek and found her asleep. She jumped up and tried to shoot me. She had a job at the factory before that, and they fired her. But she kept on working. Everybody was afraid to tell her to go away.
>
> We usually have 15 to 20 serving time in this jail. Our busy time is the Sun Dance. We make 40 or 50 arrests every day. Last year we had 179 all together. Five of them got arrested every day of the four days. The Sun Dance announcer likes to give the totals, like baseball scores.

Another investigator took me to a Nebraska town to arrange the transfer of a woman prisoner back to the reservation jail. Listen to her:

> I was away a year in Chicago in Title V training. I was going to finish high school, too. But I got hungry for meat and came back for a visit. My aunt wanted me to hock my radio. We got a gallon of wine and some hamburgers and sat on the hill. I was with my aunt and uncle and my oldest boy [twelve] and my daughter [six]. Boy, they don't drink like that in the city! That gallon was going round and round. We got to arguing about my mom not taking care of me and all, then we was on the ground fighting. That's all I remember. I don't remember cutting my wrists or nothing.
>
> Twelve years ago I cut my wrists another time. I was sober then. And another year I had a nervous breakdown. I had three kids. I got married and he accused me of

marrying to give them a name. He beat me awful. The next baby was premature. I gave her away to my cousin. The next four were by my husband. He beat me up and cut me with a bottle. I tried to kill myself a few times. Then I left him. He is in the pen now for the fifth time for grand theft. He is married again, I hear, but we ain't divorced. I gave the second baby away, too.

I've been helped before by psychiatrists. It does me a world of good to talk about myself. I'm not supposed to drink because of heart leakage. Another thing, I missed a period. It's the guy I'm going to get married to. Now that my husband is in the pen I know where he's at. The papers will go through real fast. I'll get around to it pretty soon.

My mom never loved me. When I was a year old I was dehydrated and anemic, they say. So she gave me to my grandmother. I didn't know my mother till I was eight. Then I stayed with her from the first grade on. Then she gave me away again until my dad got out of the pen. Then my grandmother beat me on the head with a shoe. Mrs. ——— took me in. She isn't a relative, I don't think. When I was thirteen they gave me to a white lady for a babysitter. I went back to school once, but I ran away and got pregnant. Then a minister and his wife adopted me. That really made me feel sad because my mother signed for it, I don't know why. Later on I was giving my dad thirty dollars a month to babysit for me. When he went to the pen for the fifth time, I had to find another babysitter. My mom won't do anything. She just draws ADC. I give her things as much as I can because I really care for her.

My aunt and uncle were in California on the relocation project. They had everything nice there, but they came back to the reservation because they were lonely. They got in a car wreck and the other person was killed. So he's sitting in jail again. The family stayed with me a whole month. I have to support them all. My car is sitting at their place, and they are selling the parts. My uncle finally got out of jail, but went right back for assault and battery. We was out of food and the baby was out of milk. Catholic Charities help me a lot when I need something real bad. There is four families near us that have come back from relocation. They are all out of food and all live in one house. It's nobody's fault but their own. No water, no bathroom. When I get out of here [jail], I'm going to hitchhike to find my children [whereabouts unknown] and get my car. If I can replace the stolen parts I can go to Omaha where it's quieter.

The Tribal Council

I had received in the mail an embossed invitation to the Sun Dance. Courtesy suggested I find the Tribal Council offices and make my formal thanks. The cordial president, Johnson Holy Rock, introduced Samuel Stands, council member, and others with lots of enthusiastic handshaking. The council is an elected body, with one member from each of the nine reservation districts plus a president and a vice president. An appointed secretary, a treasurer, and a "fifth member," along with the vice president and president, constitute the Executive Committee. The council *is* the Oglala government. It resembles, superficially, the traditional councils of older tribal times. Its function, the members said jokingly at my meeting with them, is "to oppose and be opposed by the Bureau of Indian Affairs. And one of these days we are going to set up a Bureau of White Man Affairs!"

The council funds the printing of invitations and advertising for the Sun Dance. A collection of the posters shows a variation in emphasis from year to year. In 1958, for example, the posters listed "Old Time Indian Celebration" as the main attraction, "with a sham battle honoring our Gold Star Parents." In posters of later years, "piercing and flesh offerings" were thought to have a better tourist draw. The possibility, never allowed to go unnoticed, that "the authorities might step in and prohibit it" added a valuable dramatic tension.

Settling one of my curiosities, the council members said that indeed the Sun Dance, although a sacred function, has council

22

financial support. The Chief Sun Dancer gets $150 plus food and expenses. Singers and dancers are paid $6 per day. The grounds preparations are done by prisoners and volunteers ("National Youth Corps and Mormons this year"). No clear accounting seems to be kept, certainly not revealed, about costs and income, such as fees for concessions. "This leads to arguments and accusations, but happens every year just about."

It was not a subject to dwell on. Somebody hurriedly introduced a distraction:

> Did you know that the buffalo and man [effigies on the Sun Dance center pole] change places? And turn upside down, too. Only the dancers can see it. Last year a meadowlark lit on the pole and dropped a very round rock. Strong medicine. It was given to a Catholic priest, who was afraid to touch it. So he put it in his shirt pocket and lost it. Some people take it [the Sun Dance] serious. Others say it's like Christianity before the white man came. I think a Sun Dancer nowadays is anyone who wants to earn $6 a day, knows how to act a little, and likes to eat a lot.

Jake Herman commented:

> I've been on the council for twenty years and never campaigned. My constituents just kept putting me in. But this is my last year. I gave away the election when I was up for president. I had 1,100 votes and ——— had only 179. He killed a beef, gave a big feed, and I told them to vote for him, he'd be a better president. So they did.

Tribal Court

Tribal judge Hobart Keith had a reputation as a quotable official who delighted in firing heated cannonballs in all directions, especially at state agencies and rival jurisdictions. He was salt and spice to newspaper reporters on and off the reservation. With a fearlessness born of complete ignorance, I slipped into a back seat of his courtroom to pick up the flavor of cases and procedure. Very soon quips from the judge were whizzing past my ears. I couldn't believe the first few tangential comments, but soon the aim became unmistakable. I had thought to be inconspicuous, but now grinning faces and laughter pinned me to my chair back. When the docket was finished—and damn if I would run sooner—the judge invited me to chambers. There a drumfire of challenge and commentary continued, some of it jovial, some stinging, part intended to bruise and embarrass, part to provoke thought about the ambiguities of his work and mine, part to demonstrate a fluid Latin and an erudition that covered not only legal and philosophical classics, but Voltaire, Pope, and Tacitus as well. Again and again a quotation was tossed up for identification: "You should know that! It's Thoreau! You never heard that before? It's from Macaulay!"

The courtroom was large, new, impressive, suitable to its purpose. The judge's chambers, in contrast, were jammed with indicators of a complex and vigorous personality. In a disarray that suggested constant use were fishing poles, shotguns, tackle boxes, ammunition, wading boots, truck parts, tools, and cans of paint. The library was extensive and wide-ranging. Large oil canvases, mostly portraits and full figures, stood half-realized on tripods or stacked against furniture. The judge was a painter of high and recognized talent, and his works were in demand. Like Whistler, he had a significant proclivity to running controversy with clients over long-undelivered commissions. Here the judge's skills in shuttlecock half-in-jest insults fed in, he said, to his "painter's block."

The judge was also in open war with most of South Dakota's other jurisdictions: "The Sioux Nation has sovereign rights, and this court is superior to any state office. They are populated, in any case, by a collection of bastards in every meaning of that term."

Hobart Keith was openly critical of psychiatry. It was ineffective or irrelevant, he believed, to the problems that flooded his schedule:

Here now, what would you do about this? This girl, whose name I won't mention, is in jail right now. She killed her father. She was drunk and he was drunk. And a houseful of drunks helped her do him in. He was a murderer himself. He killed his wife. He was a neighborhood bad guy, beat up his family, terrorized them and whoever else he could. They all lived in a wall tent the year round. How they got through the winters is beyond me to understand. The girl is now in jail in Nebraska. She won't talk, won't say anything, won't defend herself. The brothers say they have knives and will kill any police that go to the funeral, "just like we killed the old man. Furthermore, we'll kill anybody who comes to the courthouse." Now how can psychiatry help them or any of us in this situation? Or how about the ———— case? You don't know the ———— case? I'll get you a summary.

He didn't, but I looked it up myself. These summary notes, disguised to avoid identifying her, convey some of the hopelessness of a Sioux child in trouble.

At age eleven, Joany was placed in a state hospital for murder. The physician assigned to her was from Malaysia and had been trained in medicine abroad. He spoke limited English and no Lakota. He was impeded by Joany's refusal to speak to him at all about anything. After some weeks of impasse "she was firmly told to tell the truth or she would have to stay in the hospital for the rest of her life." She then produced an account that was recorded in the hospital chart.

Her mother was said to be slovenly, dirty, "lived like a hog," and had been jailed innumerable times for intoxication on gasoline, paint fumes, and alcohol. She was described as "a peyote user" and practitioner of "the old tribal religions." The father was described as "a fairly good Indian until he got a three-year sentence for murder." While on parole he was killed when driving while intoxicated. There were five children, Joany being the second oldest. The ADC checks were used to finance the mother's drinking. The children were all "given away, signed over" to a boarding school when Joany was eight and were never visited. Joany was a difficult and rebellious student. She often ran away. She was "sneaky, stubborn, lied constantly, and stole often." She formed close relationships only with girls younger than herself.

These she dominated by threats, and she "maintained a whip hand" over them. She was noted to "depise boys" and to nurse a hatred of other classmates. In the dormitory she was, many times, accused of undressing and abusing smaller girls, leaving them crying. The staff, however, had no first-hand observations of this and took no action. Psychiatric examination and psychological testing were recommended when Joany was nine and again when she was ten, but services were unavailable.

On the day of the murder Joany persuaded three other girls to leave the school grounds. Late in the afternoon they returned to school, saying they had been playing on a nearby swing. In the evening, a smaller child was missed and the four were questioned. At first they said they knew nothing, but after discrepancies in their stories surfaced they were again questioned. The collapse of the agreed-upon excuses soon followed. Joany then said that she had watched from a distance while the smaller child, the still-missing one, had been sexually abused by three white men. Told to show where this had happened, she instead led them to the body.

The four girls were taken to an off-reservation detention center. On the way they were taken shopping for new clothes and toys. The reasons for this odd largesse were not explained. That night Joany destroyed all of these purchases. The destruction seemed inexplicable and was left as a mystery. During observation in detention, suspicion grew that Joany was threatening the others, in Sioux, to maintain silence. A Lakota-speaking spy was placed in the holding room and in due course this story emerged.

The girls had agreed to run toward the class buildings when the morning bell rang, but then to run to the nearby trees and beyond. The victim-to-be, younger and smaller, was told she would be taken swimming. This child had made Joany angry weeks before by throwing a rock at her, and Joany had not forgotten. The five girls, unmissed at school, played on the swing for a while. Then they beat and scratched the victim and pushed her into "a hole full of oil." They threw away her shoes and took off her clothes. They then proposed to wash her, which they did, and then held her under water in the creek. Pulled out, she was scratched and cut with rocks. A stick was forced into her vagina. After this, some of the girls thought she was dead, but Joany said she was just crying. To revenge this, her eyes were held open and sand poured in and rubbed. They then covered her with mud to hide her. This was ineffective so they washed her off again. Joany then sat on her back in the water. Later the child was left in the creek while they went picking grapes. Eventually they went back to school, still not missed, and mingled with the other children.

Since Joany was oldest and the ringleader, she was sent from the detention center to an out-of-state mental hospital. The diagnosis was "adjustment reaction of childhood, conduct disturbance, but we can just about as easily think of her as a trait disturbance. Without psychiatric intervention, she can be expected to become a passive-aggressive personality." It was recommended that she leave the dormitory school. Return to the parents was "not appropriate because the mother cannot be found and the father is deceased." The final advice, that she be "rehabilitated in a federal institution and placed in a foster home" was so vague and incapable of accomplishment that the case came back to the tribal judge. "What would you do?" he demanded. "What would *you* do?"

Later, the child was sent to a southwestern state industrial school. After a few months she was returned to the custody of her mother, a homeless, severely deteriorated alcoholic. Since Joany remained "out of contact" with probation workers, attention was focused on the preparation of a detailed record of her subsequent activities—glue sniffing, fights, "disorderly conduct," and sociopathy. The child and the record had no operational connection.

School

The BIA boarding school was a pleasant but plainly appointed building where children from distant or disrupted homes lived in dormitory style. Some were very young. The teachers, for the most part, were earnestly committed and eager to discuss their work and students. Favorable first impressions led to lasting friendships, more searching discussions, and serious correspon-dence about teaching issues. I was away when an evaluation entitled "A System of Neglect: Indian Boarding Schools," was published.[1] It must have shaken their earnestness.

The school at Holy Rosary Mission had more modern class-rooms and a bright library, largely home-built and -furnished. The Jesuit fathers with whom I talked were busy publishing a series of studies on the education of Teton children. The problem focused on was keeping them in school so that the excellent curriculum (white-designed, white-taught) could achieve its pur-pose. This seemed reasonable enough, without a doubt. But we should have been filled with doubts. Did time and progress have the same meaning to Sioux children as it did to their teachers? What is the true weight to the Sioux of our best advice when *wašicu* ("white man") is said to mean "be-watchful-what-is-he-going-to-do-next," when "white man" connotes duplicity and unpredictability? Common Sioux conversation repeats and re-peats that there is a difference to be comprehended: "Our rhythms are different than yours; we can't get used to your eight-to-five ways of doing things." How do I, for example, understand a Sioux friend and coworker of many years, living in an eastern city, working at a skilled office job? She returned to university a continent away to work toward an advanced degree, and soon began to round upon me in unrelenting anger that "Indians are not allowed to make it in graduate programs." Some of us had to wait for Robert Coles's *Children of Crisis* (1977), with its insights into children growing up Indian, before we could add useful dimensions to our understanding.

Alcoholism

Pine Ridge in 1967 was a "closed reservation"—no alcohol per-mitted. But it has not been so every year since the Sioux dis-covered they could vote prohibition in or out and that they do not have to accede to BIA dictates on what is good for them. Closed or not, there are plenty of littered bottles. Pheasant Brand mus-catel is popular. Also "MD" ("Mad Dog"—Mogen David).

Stories of the daily misery caused by alcoholism abound:

Two women came in the night in the winter, crying and drunk. My wife wouldn't let them in the house. Finally, the hired man took them home. They stopped the car on the road to pee, and began to run in opposite directions. He finally got them in the car because it was so cold. One of them had picked up a piece of glass and was going to cut him. He took them to their house. They wouldn't get out of the car and wanted to go someplace else. He finally dumped them in Kyle.

In the public setting of the rodeo, drinkers grew argumentative or maudlin or both, with grandiose declamations—"Go on, Johnny, take the money and the car, but leave poor old Dad out of it!" Or, "When I get up in the morning, I slap my feet on the floor, put on my pants, and I'm a man. That's the way I was made. I can't help it!" One cowboy unable to stand or walk: "Stand back, you sonsabitches; I'll whup them all again. I'll show you who's the daddy of them all!"

Somewhere the big talk crosses the line between funny and obnoxious, and Law and Order shows up. Some of the drunks run fleetingly, dodging through the crowd, everybody laughing, even the cops. One of the undefeated feels he was called upon for an explanation: "They *told* me to act drunk, so I did!"

Cars passing through Whiteclay on the way to the reservation load up with bottles. On the reservation bootleggers are easy to find. My eye was not tuned to them, but deeply inebriated people, the assertive, the psychotic, had no problem replenishing their empties.

Working with the Mental Health Service, I was called on for emergency consultations at the jail. On one occasion, "Cornelia" had been put in the holding tank for a day because she seemed dead drunk. By the next day she was a furious, hostile, middle-aged woman shouting demands at everyone and seemingly on the verge of assaulting jailers and other prisoners and for no evident reason. The questions were: Is she insane? Does she need to go up to the hospital? In an interrogation room I was introduced to her and within moments had no hesitation in agreeing with the previous diagnosis—she was certainly angry! She shouted at me threateningly. She said she wanted nothing to do with me. It was time for her to be released, she said, and, goddammit, get on with it. Harsh expletives and obscene recommendations flowed from her with enthusiasm, and gestures with her fists.

Suddenly she broke off this tirade and said she had taken an overdose of medication given to her somewhere on prescription. She wouldn't say what medication or what physician had prescribed it, or how much she had taken. She was angry, she said, and felt fully justified in spitting rage because she was accused of being a drunk. "I'm *not* a drunk! I work hard. I live with my brother and his four kids" (abandoned by their alcoholic mother). She felt intolerably harassed by her (separated) husband, who kept after her to pay bills, which took up all her allotment money and her wages. He kept hinting at a breakup between them, which she didn't want. She had had a "good marriage," except for his drinking, for the past sixteen years. Further, she mourned her father, who had died three years before, and she said she wanted yearningly to be buried with him. Further still, she couldn't sleep and was nervous. And her alcoholic mother had gone off to a four-day dance, leaving her to care for the four children. Finally, she had been discharged from a tuberculosis hospital, where she had had four months of medication for "nervous breakdown."

There was no follow-up. It had not occurred to her to go back to her physician there. She had thought, and now decided to voice it as a threat, to begin drinking like her mother and her husband—"It's the only way to stay healthy!" She made several ingenious anatomical suggestions as to what I could do with a proposed appointment at the local hospital or the hospital she had but recently left (against medical advice). She was as angry on departure as on my arrival, insisted she had committed no crime and could secure her discharge from the jail as soon as I got out of her way.

Or consider the case of another woman, age thirty-four but looking fifty-four, who had walked away from a nursing home where she was a long-time resident because she felt lonely. She was picked up by a police van when the driver saw her sitting alone on the side of the road, drinking wine. In jail, four days later, she was an uncombed, noncommittal woman in an old blue dress and broken shoes. She laughed or grinned secretively and gave a sparse and confusing description of herslf with frequent reversals or contradictions. She said she had two husbands and a son who was older than she was, but it seemed more confused than riddling. She wanted out of jail but insisted she needed nothing else. "Besides, nothing can be done." She said she wanted to go home (but couldn't say where home was) because her son had been killed in Rapid City and they were going to have a funeral tomorrow. She had, she said, sixteen other children. It was only from other sources that I learned she had been in Yankton State Hospital four times without improvement or any prospect of it. She had lived, briefly, in many different nursing homes arranged for her by various agency workers. She was basically nomadic, long an alcoholic, possibly retarded, possibly schizophrenic. She had assisted her husband in beating her father to death. No one could enumerate her children or their where-abouts.

The Suicide Road

The narrow blacktop between Pine Ridge Town and Whiteclay, Nebraska, is string straight but vertically undulant. Visibility is shallow. "No passing" signs are frequent. With but reasonable care any innocent might believe he was safe. At one end is a cluster of wide-open saloons. At the other end strict prohibition reigns, irregularly. The topography has an attractiveness to high-speed drivers, who feel they are on rails, with the up-and-down thrills of a roller coaster. Add alcohol and the Whiteclay road is a special statistic. The suicide rate on all American Indian reserva-tions is astoundingly high—several times the overall national rate. Researchers ascribe it to economic and identity frustra-tions, to the frozen-in-place atmosphere in which the Indian people live. The Mental Health Clinic explored another inven-tion, the moratorium theory, which proposed that some individ-uals need to go out of business briefly—on a psychological vacation, so to say—and that death is not the aim, although often the inadvertent accomplishment. A fearfully mangled survivor I knew at the V.A. clinic told me, "I got good and drunk and went back and forth to Whiteclay as fast as I could until I found somebody to head-on with me."

The Pine Ridge Drugstore

"Lakota Pejuta Tipi" (*Lakʿota Pʿejuta Tʿípi*), "Sioux Drugstore," says the sign in front. The drugstore, on the main street, is fortresslike, with heavy door and window bars. Business is light and the hours are limited. The proprietor seems glad to see a white face. He spends as much time as he can in Rapid City with his family, and is frank to say he is afraid of Indians. He doesn't like to be afraid and he hates the reservation. Why stay?

A First Look at the Economy

Go drive the roads of South Dakota and Nebraska. A few transects make clear that the reservation boundary is an ecological as well as a segregational line. Arid ranges and clay deserts in the rain shadow of the Black Hills were allocated to the hunting tribes, the watered valleys to the homesteaders. The valleys are now richly productive and of great expanse. The ranges and deserts, cleared of game, are as parched as ever. Survey teams and boundary commissions had exercised remarkable agronomic foresight and only one correction was necessary. It appeared, in practice, that a rectangle between Batesland and Mission, using today's maps, could be profitably cultivated. It was excised from the reservation in 1911 and put on tax roles as Bennett County. The division between farmable and nonfarmable being thus established, the Oglalas were urged to become useful, self-sufficient farmers on the Euro-American model. They were inherently averse to day labor in the white tradition, and contemptuous, in their own long tradition, of the farming tribes to the east. They had believed, naively, as was soon clear, that subsistence was guaranteed by treaty. Many agreed to try dryland

32

cultivation after rations were reduced and the threat of starvation became a grim reality. Nevertheless, those Sioux who went along with the forced transformation of hunters to field workers lacked the techniques, customs, incentives, and equipment of an agricultural people. They were soon crushed by the weather, their own incompetence, drought, grasshoppers, and inadequate capitalization. Many contemporary white farmers of the new West were crushed, not as quickly but in the same ways and for the same reasons. Cattle and horse raising were tried next. Better suited to the rangeland and more consistent with the Indians' experience, but without an operational marketing structure, these ventures were promising at first, disappointing later, and eventually collapsed.

Today the Oglalas, with few exceptions, are neither ranchers nor farmers, but merely occasionally employed migrants living at the bottom of the poverty scale. The land is used, some of it, by white ranchers who have become skilled at the high-risk production of large-acreage wheat and barley combined with holdings of cattle, hay, and pasturage. Such ventures depend on extensive mechanization and borrowed capital beyond the reach of the small holder. The Oglalas lease their remaining land to these multiparceled operations. Estimates suggest the Oglalas had an average annual family income in 1967 of less than two thousand dollars, which some augmented by migrant labor or government jobs. Goods and services provided by the United States government under treaty—food commodities, education, housing, health care—cost about eight thousand dollars per household per year. It is difficult to measure what the value is to the recipient families, but certainly nothing approaching eight thousand dollars. The people remain profoundly poor. Reservation unemployment runs from 40 to 85 percent. There is no bank at Pine Ridge or in the districts; there is little money in pockets or investments, and little reason for white-operated agencies or businesses to use an on-reservation banking institution while dependable ones flourish in every off-reservation town.

Between largely conservative full-blood and largely modernizing mixed-blood factions there is little popular support for the political system. Few people vote. It is difficult, in fact next to impossible, to organize consistent community support for farming development, industry, or tourism. Several small projects (an irrigation district and a cattle-production cooperative) have survived, but remain at pilot stage. One successful Brulé Sioux cattle rancher told me:

> It is impossible for an Indian to succeed in a money economy. He has to feed his relatives. Everything is given away even if it's mortgaged. He gets a farm loan and the fence posts go into the wood stove, the wire is sold for gas money, and he invites all his relatives in to barbeque the breeding stock. Anyhow, an Indian can't get a loan if he has an Indian name, and if he's got a white name, even then it's only maybe.

Where do reservation groceries come from? In part, from country stores, many miles apart, all small, all run by whites. I was told: "An Oglala couldn't possibly run a store. His family and in-laws wouldn't expect to pay for anything. Cousins would come from Los Angeles and Chicago to live off him till the shelves were empty. And people who couldn't say they were relatives would borrow him to death."

White store owners tend to be elderly, and some are second-generation in the business, even so. They operate at bare-existence levels in turn-of-the-century buildings. Each has boxes and closets stuffed with native crafts, a museum of slowly decaying treasures in clothing, beadwork, headresses, dance costumes, all left long ago to secure small purchases of food or gasoline. Proprietors have pledged not to sell heirlooms. Sometimes, on long acquaintance, they pull out bulky cartons full of unpaid bills. Custom demands that dignified, cash-poor patrons be carried for long periods, for life sometimes, and storekeepers don't expect to balance their books.

In 1965 Wounded Knee had one of the oldest of the country general stores, with an Indian trading post atmosphere. Under a low ceiling on a splintered wooden floor were a post office, a grocery store, variety goods, craft supplies, and a long counter piled deep with old-tradition moccasins, buckskin dresses covered with elk teeth, drums, and weapons. The discerning shopper could find, for example, medicine bags of protohistoric date, yet also purchase, at the other end of the store, canned peaches and black fishnet stockings. "Cultural diffusion" is the term, I think.

Clyde Gildersleeve came to North Dakota and Montana from Iowa in the early 1900s. He worked as a cowboy out of Glendive, came to Porcupine in 1910 to be a trader, and to Wounded Knee in 1914 as postmaster and trader. He told me: "In those times the roads were dirt. The doctors came to the house when people were sick. Even through snowstorms, riding horseback with the mail carrier. When the PHS [Public Health Service] came, they wouldn't make house calls. Anyway, I've been here since 1914 running this store. Married a Chippewa woman and made my life here." A few years after this conversation, Clyde was to take on younger partners, both off-reservation whites. The old store was replaced by a new concrete-slab, steel-beamed building. An entrance-fee museum was built, and a new, hard-nosed policy about credit introduced. Both buildings were destroyed during Wounded Knee II.

The white economy functioning on the reservation deserves more than an impressionistic sketch. Serious documentation might begin with Gordon Macgregor's *Warriors without Weapons* (1946), E. E. Hagan's *On the Theory of Social Change: How Economic Growth Begins* (1962), and Raymond DeMallie's "Pine Ridge Economy: Cultural and Historical Perspectives" (1978). Also revealing are Joseph Jorgensen's *The Sun Dance Religion: Power for the Powerless* (1972); André Frank's *Capitalism and Underdevelopment in Latin America* (1967), which is as pertinent to the concept of North American reservations as it is to third-world colonies; and David F. Aberle's "The Sun Dance and Reservation Underdevelopment" (1973), an eloquent essay on deprivation and exploitation as a regular function of the larger politico-economic structure.

As a tragicomic description of the day-to-day operation of the reservation cash economy there is a tenderhearted appraisal by

Dan Cushman in *Stay Away, Joe.* Caucasian ranchers, who find this novel both accurate and funny, are equipped by long experience to give variations on the theme. Orville Schwarting, for example, who ran four thousand cattle on lease land; grew wheat, barley, and alfalfa; and lived on the Red Shirt drainage, told me this story:

Old ———— was into me three years ahead of his lease. Five dollars here, ten dollars there, until I blew up at him. Then he wanted to increase his land fee. I told him, "You can make a lot more. Farm it yourself." Course he didn't want to do that. He came to the door last February and wanted fifteen dollars to bury his son. The boy had run across the creek on the ice, broke through, and drowned. He said, "If you think this is just another hard luck story, come out to the car. I got him froze stiff as a post in the back seat."

Let me tell you! Barbara ———— is a leaseholder. She called up collect to say she was stranded in Spearfish. She offered thirty dollars off the lease money if somebody would come get her. I got two of her relatives and went up there. She was not at home. Her bedding was at her boarding house with ninety dollars owed on her rent. We searched the bars and found her drunk, with a boy friend. She said, "Oh, I'll be ready after a while. Or come back tomorrow." We finally got away by paying thirty dollars against her bill. On the way home she started running up the highway in the dark. Next, her relatives wouldn't let her in the house. Then her boy friend tried to take the car. He was just out of the penitentiary.

Actually, seriously, Indians have too small an economic base—too little land in one piece, too little interest in qualifying for FHA or any other loans. As a hired hand they want three days off a week and never work on Saturday or Sunday. So they can never make it farming. Always have to go to town to Welfare or something. They lease their land to whites because whites pay top dollar and are more dependable. They know better than to lease to another Indian. Never would get their money. Ranching requires more capital, more risk, and more dedication than they're willing to put into it. Capital loans have been available to them and still are. Some have good gardens for a while, if they put their minds to it. But then they seem to forget how to do it. The initiative seems to go out of it.

He stared when I asked if the Sioux are getting even by being passive.

Oglalas speak of poverty as the result of broken treaties, unrelenting white deception, and fraud practiced upon national minorities. It follows from that argument that corrective measures will entail more and more payments, preferably in cash. White ranchers assert great value in hard work, self-reliance, and freedom from government interference (while meticulously manipulating farm-subsidy programs). They see reservation poverty as devolving expectedly from a bureaucracy that fosters dependency and grows worse year by year. As one Oglala commented: "The Indian spends his day going from agency to agency, arranging for them to find him a job, a bank loan, commodity food, and clothing; collect his lease money; give him some breeding stock and gas money. At 5 P.M., he's tired. He goes for a beer while the agencies try to figure out what they are going to do for him tomorrow."

Visits in the Country

August 15: Kills-in-Water wanted to go visit Mrs. Oliver Moose because she had a very old pipe to sell. She lived in a log cabin at the end of a dirt road. The inside was scrubbed almost white—irregular plank floors and a drooping muslin ceiling. Mrs. Moose was a gentle, hospitable lady of seventy-nine and she did indeed have a pipe to sell. She slowly unpacked a large trunk of treasures and found the pipe—two pipes indeed—but they were very small catlinite "woman's pipes" about an inch long. One was broken. She also had a well-worn knife in beaded sheath "from the

Wounded Knee battle" (as all old knives for sale are said to be). What she most wanted us to see was an album of early pictures. One was of a relative, a middle-aged man who had not had pictures made during his life, so his coffin was tipped upright and a portrait was made the day of his funeral. He was dressed in a suit solidly beaded, mostly in white, from chin to ankles, coat and trousers, cuffs and lapels, vest and necktie.

I went by on a courtesy call another year. She was not at home. She had gone to the Sun Dance by team and wagon, many miles cross-prairie.

August 19: With a Social Service worker I went looking for Siefert Young Bear, one of the rangers. The country was very green because of recent rains. There were great fields of sunflowers blooming, and pink cleome, then a small group of cabins miles beyond Porcupine on a dirt road. A group of kids stared at us but stayed mute. A woman said, lethargically, "He's gone," which we could see. An old man in a black suit sat in a tent drumming and singing. He gave no answers to our questions either. The field worker thought it was because of rustling trouble lately—"Makes people afraid to talk if they don't know you." On the way back we passed the place where Big Foot and his people were picked up by the army the day before the Wounded Knee massacre.

August 28: Stopped at Sharp's Corner, where the storekeeper advised: "Why don't you talk to Lucie Looks Twice? She's Black Elk's daughter. She can tell you a lot about *yuwipi*. Look up Afraid of Hawk and Underbaggage and the Pretty Hip family. And Lillian Tobacco; she fixes dry meat and digs wild turnips and knows how to find them."

2. Oglala Concepts of Power

Oglala healers with few exceptions are those senior men and women who come to practice late in life, when accumulated knowledge and experience would normally place them in advisory positions in their communities. Most are men, women tending to specialize in herbalism or perhaps in the sex-specific ailments of females. The medicine men who are the subject of this book are ritualists whose elaborate ceremonies, derived from visionary powers, promote health and well-being; they are healers of physical and psychological sickness whose tools are sacred songs and ritual actions as well as herbal and other more mundane treatments. Some are born into families endowed with medical or ritual skill, but the healing calling itself hinges upon the intensity of individual conviction derived from dream or vision. Healing ability is thought of and spoken of as beyond human control and ambition. Medical *training* is a phrase without relevance. *Preparation,* on the other hand, encompasses all of the life of the healer. Wisdom is the prerequisite. There are no eager young graduates fresh from formal education. Some Lakotas have heard of Caucasian-supported schools for medicine men among the Navajos,[1] but they do not envisage such schools for themselves. The idea appears to them to be conceptually unsound.

Healers learn song and ceremony with recognized mentors. Medicine bundles and ceremonial programs containing powers of the supernatural may be bequeathed or purchased, but more often the aspirant attends older ritualists as an assistant singer or drummer for many years. He may, in addition, participate repeatedly in the Sun Dance and other rites, gathering powers and reputation. Beyond these, the essential achievements reside in the development of a sense of personal ritual competence, the garnering of spiritual helpers, the belief that one can safely represent the spirit world to humankind, and the accumulated confidence and assertiveness to present oneself as effective. In practice, of course, results matter. Successes are recounted oratorically, like prowess in battle, and reputations grow or wither. The aspect of authority is always critical. It has been said that authority in Western medical practice may derive from lay deference and the institutionalized dependency of the patient as much as or more than it does from scientific knowledge. It is certain that the Oglala healer devotes as much attention to the careful nurturance of client attitudes as do his non-Indian counterparts.

A healing session is never a casual encounter. It is arranged through a formalized approach procedure after discussion by the patient with family, advisers, or intermediaries. Unhurried discussion of all implications of the problem in and by the community is often a preliminary. It is essential that the healer, the physical or symbolic disorder, and the proposed treatment procedure appear to stand in a harmonious relationship before the applicant sends an emissary or goes himself on a formal "carrying of the pipe" to the medicine man. Several initiating visits may be needed to establish a workable contact. Acceptance by the healer is followed by instructions on preliminary actions, which may include fasting, vision seeking, abstinences, prayers, or the preparation of offerings or feasts. The acceptance obligates the healer to a full commitment to the problem and to selection of the ceremony and schedule. The patient now has an alliance he can depend upon. The medicine man may seek information from the client's family, acquaintances, tribal offices, and others. As in many small towns, he may know about the issues before the client arrives for the first visit and may use his knowledge to promote corrective measures across a wide community spectrum.

40

Indigenous healers proceed as if they have in mind the principles used by physicians in many other cultures—that time is often an ally in recovery, fears and passions fade, problems pass, neglect sometimes suffices, all therapeutics help at first or to some degree, placebos are not inert, and patients often get well irrespective of theory and in spite of practice. They know that the presence of the physician itself arouses hope and palliates fear. Healers repeatedly affirm the patient's tribal identity and sense of belonging.

The healers' ritual is the night sing (*lowaŋpi*), a dramatic production. It has a stage, music, and actors. As in a play, the audience is encouraged to suspend ordinary reality in the service of a new experience. Darkness, immobility, and the weight of heavy repeated sound (quite apart from the content and sequence of songs and prayer) promote a selective sensory overload combined with sensory deprivation. Incongruities come to be ignored, imagination is stimulated, and the barriers between dreaming and waking are attenuated. The manipulation on stage of symbolic objects and ideas tends to reinforce archetypal traditions. All encourage the mind to open to a world inhabited by the dead, the ancestors, the spirits, and the gods.

The assessment of the value and results of ritual treatment has to be made from an indigenous rather than a laboratory viewpoint. The Oglala healer and his clients are more inclined to think that the process of indirect contemplation, naming, and ceremony are ends in themselves. Some of the functions of healing-by-ritual apply to individual client-patients, others to their relationship to family, band, and tribe. The medicine men use an orotund oratorical style as though their words themselves are magical instruments, driving an accelerating circular reinforcement, entraining feeling and thought. Their speech moves back and forth over the issues at hand, reorganizing and restating the past and present and the details and the whole. At the end the discourse emphasizes the coherence of natural and supernatural worlds and the introjection of this continuity and harmony into the intrapsychic universe.

In the presentations concerning individual medicine men I

hope to be able to convey some of the pleasure of working with them and some of the colorfulness of their personalities and the settings within which they operate. At the same time I ask the reader to attend with me to the dynamics of their behavior. Why is it that the clients seem to grant the healer a greater wisdom and authority, even in matters that they might otherwise deal with casually and competently themselves? Is this surrender of autonomy motivated simply by the expectation of greater good to come? Do the patients or clients await in return a richer comprehension of themselves and their world, a better integration of inner and outer experience, a diminution of anxiety, and enhancement of self-value?

These achievements are sometimes sought in Western psychotherapy and we may ask as we go along if they have parallels in ritual experience. Another analogy with at least some psychotherapies is the patient's willingness and even eagerness to suspend critical judgment. Participants in ritual demonstrate unwonted suggestibility and participate voluntarily in illusion. In night sings, for example, the flashing blue sparks are obviously produced by a wheel-and-flint cigarette lighter. The shaman and audience, however, identify the lights as manifestations of spirit helpers. "The spirits make the lights," says the medicine man, and we all agree, "Huh!" It is not an "as if" or a "representation of" but an identification, and is accepted at that level.

For comparison, recall that off-stage sounds in a play may be taken by the audience to suggest thunder but not to literally portend rain within the theater. The suspension of disbelief may be highly selective, as when a participant speaks disdainfully the next day about the clumsy performance of the shaman's conjuring or describes his amusement at the accidental betrayal in the stage management of the mysteries, without any loss in his belief in the effectiveness of the ritual as a whole.

The remainder of this chapter introduces Sioux concepts of ritual power and methods of evoking it through the pipe ceremony, the preparatory functions of *inipi* (purification), and the vision quest. All are fundamental to an understanding of the shamanic healing procedures of the medicine men of Pine Ridge.

The Wak'aŋ

Oglala ceremonial life is based upon the quest for supernatural power (*sic'uŋ*). The word *wak'aŋ* has intricate connotations but in many of its usages it is equivalent with power or source of power. *Wak'aŋ* is the awesome, the unknowable, the ineffable, the expansive universal All, the sacred and the holy, the Great Mystery. *Wak'aŋ* can become conditionally manifest in persons, creatures, and things, but it is fundamentally an attribute of the supernatural. The *wak'aŋ* is the space occupied by the dead and by their condensations into named benevolent and evil beings. Oglala ritual is organized so as to make power manifest and to facilitate its transmission to people. When humankind is defined in the course of ritual as submissive, sacrificial, and impotent, a favorable gradient of *wak'aŋ* flow is increased. *Wak'aŋ* power is inherently dangerous and it may also assume an explicit evil (*síca*) aspect.

It follows that its management must be the demarcated province of the adept, the medicine man. It is he who endlessly reinforces the crucial human delusion that death is escapable. The dead are not dead but remain alive in a special manner as spirits, ghosts, or souls, and are domiciled in a separate world to which the shaman-priest has access and serves as courier. It is to his advantage that the affects of death are conserved and transformed into the terror and awe with which we clothe the gods.

The search for power, from the viewpoint of individual psychology, begins with the basic needs for security and sustenance that underlie children's striving for physical and cognitive mastery of the surrounding world. These shape their development in adaptive directions. The search for omnipotence is an extension of the process. Magical thought seeks omnipotent control of objects at a distance, religious thought seeks to find salvation by identification with omnipotent entities, scientific thought by accumulation of knowledge through observation, experiment, and verification. Healers in all cultures seem to require a strong sense of personal omnipotence, which perhaps serves to stabilize competence.

The Pipe

The medicine pipe is the principal sacred object mediating the exchanges between humans and the *wak'aŋ*. The antiquity of the use of the sacred pipe in the New World is attested by numerous pre-Columbian representations, with equally sacred tobacco, in Mayan and Aztecan iconography.[2] For the Oglalas, the pipe is identified literally with the original sacred pipe, the gift of the shape-changing, supernatural White Buffalo Woman who brought codes of moral behavior, power, and survival to the Sioux. The White Buffalo Woman story, common to all divisions of the Teton Sioux, describes the creation of religion. Her sacred bundle exists still, and is preserved by *wak'aŋ* guardians along with its associated legends and rituals.[3]

Pipes used today are made by several reservation craftsmen—Robert Morrison (Holy Dance) was one, George Swift Bird another—or are imported as finished items, rough blanks, or bulk stone from the quarries in Minnesota. Some beautiful pipes of greenstone, soapstone, black slate, or other substances are seen at Sun Dances, but most are made of red catlinite. The classic plain pipes with elongate and fragile bowl and stem are smoothly polished objects with great aesthetic appeal. The basic inverted T shape may be augmented with carving, engraving, or inlays. The stem is properly of ash, a hardwood with a suitable pith cavity. Sumac is less valued, easier to obtain and work but soft and coarse and given to checking and splitting. The stem may be slender and simple, or carved more or less ornately, or covered with quill work, feather work, or beading. A pipe made for me by Holy Dance has a heavy catlinite bowl and a thirty-two-inch stem wrapped in red cloth. Another, which he used himself, had a bison carved in full-round on the stone forestem. Another, given as a gift at a leavetaking ceremony, had a fifteen-inch stem decorated with a burned design of lines and diamonds, and a small bowl. A venerable woman at Porcupine showed me two women's pipes, the catlinite bowls L-shaped and less than an inch long.

As a sacred object, the pipe may be kept in a quilled, beaded, or painted buckskin bag, the stem and bowl separated. Accessory items are the tobacco pouch or gourd, and a carved, polished chokecherry-wood reamer-tamper eight inches long and pointed at one end. A used Sun Dance skewer is sometimes treasured for use as a pipe tamper. The pipe bag may be ornately decorated with a long fringed and quilled addition. A pipe is sometimes kept in a wrapped bundle with other ritual paraphernalia where it may not be smoked for decades or generations. The pipe is made sacred by the prayers of the medicine man. Most formally this is accomplished at a sweat lodge ritual. Less formally, the pipe becomes sacred as the medicine man addresses it, picks it up, gestures with it, or uses it in the prefatory prayers of any ritual: the vision quest preparations, the Sun Dance, Making Relatives, Ghost Keeping, Throwing the Ball, and Buffalo Sing (maiden's puberty ritual). The pipe may be used in almost any context to convey a message of importance. "Carrying the pipe" may be either a figure of speech or an actual gesture. To present oneself in a formal way may include "carrying the pipe to" some person, meeting, or power. To initiate an important request, to make a situation "proper" in all senses, to connote integrity, morality, sincerity, or matters of ancestral or traditional significance, one "carries the pipe."

The ubiquitousness of the pipe as the accompaniment of portentous acts or thoughts has brought about some dilution of its original meanings. The decorations of Christian churches on the reservation sometimes include actual pipes or their representations in paintings, embroidery, or altar decorations. At the end of the Sun Dance of 1969, a Catholic service given near the Sun Dance pole included an altar with a white cloth cover, silver chalice, and two pipes held bowl-opposite-bowl to form a cross. The syncretism of the pipe with Christ and the cross has been much developed in reservation Catholic liturgy, albeit in the face of the criticism that is so common in Sioux social processes.

Wakiyuza, the gestures of the pipe ceremony, are subject to infinite variation and interpretation, depending on the occasion and on the styles of individual medicine men. The essentials, each portion accompanied by prayer and song, are the opening of

the pipe bundle, fitting the bowl and stem, filling the bowl, and addressing the six directions before and after lighting. Meticulous rules govern the passing of the pipe (sometimes with four ritual repetitions), carrying of the pipe (sunwise, that is, clockwise, although counter directions also may be given significance on occasion), placing of the pipe on altars, lighting the pipe, refilling it, and retiring of the pipe from the sacred space. Phrases uttered while passing the pipe are *Hau ate* ("Greetings, father") and *Tʿuŋkaśila Wakʿaŋ Tʿáŋka* ("Grandfather, Great Mystery").

Tobacco is both a sacred and a profane substance. Its sacred use is controlled by all the ritual structures pertinent to the *wakʿaŋ*. Smoking for pleasure seldom includes the medicine pipe or aboriginal forms of tobacco, although on occasion their use may connote a contemplative or meditative mood. Tobacco used ritually is called "kinnikinnick" or "Indian tobacco" in bland disregard that it comes from the trader's store in the familiar white cloth bags labeled "Bull Durham."

A substitute for tobacco, or an addition to it, may be the dried leaves of bearberry (*Arctostaphylos uva-ursi*), broken up by rolling between the palms, and the shaved inner bark of the red willow (*Cornus stolonifera*). The former is a recumbent plant of the mountains; the latter grows in thickets along creeks, where its bright red bark adds color to otherwise drab winter landscapes. Both are called "kinnikinnick." Other additives are also spoken of. One is alleged to be hallucinogenic and is irregularly obtainable on the Standing Rock Reservation. Another is a trade item "from Montana," *c⁽aŋli icahiye,* which I discuss more fully in Chapter 6. It is commonly sold at country stores or at dance gatherings in the form of a dried woody root. Fine shavings of it are added to tobacco and impart a faintly licorice flavor and odor reminiscent of sweet cicely (*Umbelliferae*). It is infrequently called Sweet Ann root. On two occasions I was able to buy "genuine Indian tobacco, real kinnickinick" on the reservation. Both samples were commercial aromatic pipe tobaccos. "Real tobacco" is also called "Cree twist." The leaves of squaw currant (*Rhus trilobata*), a common prairie shrub, are also used as a base or additive for smoking mixtures.

Purification

Inikaġapi, the sweat lodge ritual, is of dual nature; it may be held either as preparatory to other rites or with its own self-contained significance. The medicine man may undertake an *inikaġapi* to consecrate a medicine pipe or to purify and prepare himself to conduct the Sun Dance or other rituals. Participants or initiates may accompany him or undergo the *inikaġapi* under his tutelage before a vison quest or before the Sun Dance.

A sweat lodge framework often identifies a South Dakota farmyard as Sioux. The wickiup-like structure is constructed of slender poles, butt ends set in the earth and tops bent over and tied to form an inverted bowl. In keeping with many Oglala explanations, the poles are said to number sixteen (four times four, a quadruple sacred number) or twenty-four (four times the sacred six directions) or twenty-eight (the "ideal number" for a Sun Dance lodge or a medicine wheel). I have never seen a lodge actually so constructed; practicality overrides ritual numbers. Commonly, one or two rows of horizontal bracing poles are bent around and tied to the uprights. The poles may be of willow or cottonwood cut from a thicket of suitable saplings.

The framework is covered with overlapped pieces of tarpaulin, blankets, or star quilts, leaving a crawl-in entryway closed with a movable door flap. The interior is nearly dark when the flap is in place and is closely sealed off from the outer air. Near the lodge is a fire pit where burning billets of wood form a bed and cover for a layer of rounded boulders. The fire tender with a shovel or fork takes instruction from the medicine man, passing heated rocks or containers of water into the lodge as called for.

In my experience, at least, the Lakotas take poker-faced pleasure in introducing a novice to the sweat lodge. It is described to him as a nearly unendurable experience, with intense heat, severe discomfort, and suffocating clouds of steam. He is warned that he will most likely burst through the walls in a desperate convulsive escape. His half-dozen or so companions discuss without encouragement his lack of bodily strength and endurance. When the moment comes to begin, the medicine man conducts an opening prayer with raised pipe. The men crawl through the low doorway and sit in darkness in a cramped circle. Some are naked, some in underwear. The rough poles of the framework have a sufficiency of sharp protuberances for the bare skin to find in the dark. In the center, much too close, is a shallow pit. This is filled with hot boulders passed in by the fire tender. He seems to have no care that the stones are radiant with heat, and appears to manipulate his long-handled shovel with careless violence. Someone cautiously jiggles the stones into position in the pit, using a heavy stick. The medicine man leads a pipe ceremony, and the pipe is passed—*"Hau ate! Hau t'uŋkasila! Ohaŋ! Ohaŋ!"* ("Greetings, father! Greetings, grandfather! Yes! Yes!")

The lodge door is closed and sacred songs begin. Water from a bucket is splashed on the stones. Steam is invisible in the dark but almost solid to the other senses. Breathing becomes difficult. Some men groan or gasp. The singing and prayers go on. To the initiate who has not yet grasped the structure of the ceremony or the sequence of the prayer and song it can seem monotonous, endless. At last a pause and the bottom edge of the lodge cover is lifted, admitting welcome coolness for a few moments until the second sprinkling of the stones begins. Through this, and the third and fourth periods, the medicine songs continue. Some of the men join in. Others whisper or shout *"Ohaŋ"* when they gather a bit of air. At intervals a water dipper is passed or, incredibly, more hot stones are handed in.

At the end of the fourth sweat the door is opened and the participants crawl out to scrub themselves with their shirts or handfuls of the sage that has carpeted the lodge. They dress, pray again, and the pipe ceremony is repeated. The ritual is now complete.

Few of the participants say much, but the medicine man is explicit that the hours have been *wak'aŋ*, that we have passed from the ordinary world to the realm of mystery. The words are his, not mine. He speaks in sacred language while I try to describe the experience to myself. A model of four ritual deaths and four resurrections comes to mind. The timeless period (was it really hours?), enervation from heavy perspiration, and the discomfort give a sense of great change. My explanations to myself were evidently incomplete, for I repeatedly redreamed my first experience without adding much to my sense of understanding.

The Vision Quest

Haŋblec'eya, "Crying for a vision," is an ancient ritual. From a psychological perspective, it may be seen as designed to satisfy the yearning for personal identity and direction at the threshold of adulthood. Magical assistance in the form of hallucinated companions and of amulets was expected to emerge, to supplement thereafter the individual's identity and direction. The crier for a vision placed himself in isolation and discomfort to evoke, with fasting, exposure, and self-torture, a mystic new experience. He placed himself as fully as he could in the other world of gods and spirits, where human loneliness and vulnerability, the presence of the fearsome unknowable, opened the soul to the *wak'aŋ*. The process required four days, at least in ritual description. In practice it depended upon the arrival of the dreamed or hallucinated vision.

Commonly a rite of male adolescence, the vision quest was

(and is) embarked upon by men or women of any age. Adults might repeat the experience, even with regularity, to strengthen resolve in war or occupation, to improve healing skills, or to achieve increments of confidence. A herbalist might cry for a vision before the ritual gathering of plants, a leader might look for prestige or decisions, or—in recent times—politicians "vision quest" for campaign purposes. The *haŋblec'eya* is without exception included in the medicine men's accounts of their personal preparation and professional competence. Fools Crow talked of yearly fasts on Bear Butte. Peter Catches lived his vision quest experience by confining himself to a remote cabin where, he said, "The soul might constantly expand in the presence of natural beauty." Shamans regularly speak of fasting, meditation, and abstentions in the service of increasing holiness apart from formal vision questing.

The *haŋblec'eya* is still practiced and vision quest sites are still strewn with offerings. Shamans still conduct the preparatory rituals and interpret the experience in terms of the *wak'aŋ*. People continue to question themselves and their roles in life, still have apprehensions, still hunger for inspiration. The dream experience and the procedures to evoke it are thought not only holy but also peculiarly individual. The privacy of the quest is respected and guarded. Secrecy is protective until there is motivation to reveal the inner life.

One aspect of the vision quest that has never been made explicit is that it exists on a continuum of experience, from the explicit ritual to the less-than-mystic processes of thought ordinarily phrased as "the idea came to me," "I decided," or "I was inspired to." Between these poles are the common Sioux acts of fasting to arrive at otherwise difficult decisions, meditation to achieve some contact with the *wak'aŋ*, night dreaming to provide material for use in prophecy and action, and the figure of speech "I had the vision to ——" as a means of expressing in quasimystic terms the accumulated rationalizations of daily life.

For several summers I camped on the prairie a half mile from Fools Crow's cabin. We exchanged meals and visits and many leisurely conversations. Visitors came and went and feasted on chokecherries and buffalo berries in their season. We settled into a profound sense of the great quiet country, learned its plants, and had the ghostly visits of the range stock in the night. The moon passed in its course a conical hill to the south called the *paha wak'aŋ,* the sacred hill. On its slopes by sunlight could be found thousands of weathered cloth-bound tobacco offerings and a scattering of rusting knives. The hill became a familiar part of our landscape and we missed it when we left in the fall, so much that I journeyed back to photograph it when I should have been doing more important things. On the top was a silent meditating figure, blanket-wrapped, motionless.

The psychodynamics of crying for a vision suggest that it is in important ways a phenomenon of identity seeking and youth. But it is by no means confined to youth or to males. Oglalas value the direction giving of their Other World. The vision quest answers the recurrent question "What do I want to be, to devote myself to?" The conditions of the rite seem to force a statement from the unconscious, to plumb what is essential in character and experience and to submit the cryptic results to the interpretation of a tutelary shaman. In modern life, identity formation is served, in part, by the school career adviser and the job-aptitude test, but Sioux children still hear about and heed the vision quest as guidance and the medicine man as a counselor.

3. The Sun Dance

The great public ritual of the Sun Dance (*Wiwaŋyag wac'ipi*) in midsummer was and is the most complex manifestation of the Oglala ritual cycle. In the month when the chokecherries ripen and when the moon rises as the sun is going down, the candidates and mentors were selected, instructions given, and preliminary sweat baths and vision quests undertaken. The scattered bands gathered in one great camp and the Sun Dance lodge and arbors were built. The Sun Dance pole was selected, cut, and re-erected in the dance circle, decorated with buffalo, man, and eagle effigies. Offerings of tobacco, cloth, and human flesh were made. The eight ritual days gave opportunity for visiting of relatives, courtships, minor rituals, and feasting. Those who had vowed sacrificial activities underwent the torture of piercing, the exhaustion of fasting, and the physical stress of prolonged dancing while gazing at the sun. The larger purposes of the ceremony centered on global ideas of benefit to the tribe; more personal aspirations dealt with the accretion of spiritual power. Sun Dance time was an intense reaffirmation of tribal and group identity.

The traditional Oglala Sun Dance is described most fully by James R. Walker.[1] It was a midsummer celebration in the period of food abundance. The urgency of the spring hunts was past, the gathering of winter provisions was not yet begun, and the people had leisure to congregate. Four preliminary days were given to pleasure—visiting, feasting, courting. Some of the austere Oglala codes of social interaction were relaxed. After the fourth evening, a solemnity appropriate to the coming four sacred days prevailed. On the second day the principal shaman mentor, accompanied by scouts, ritually sought a suitable cottonwood tree as if it were an enemy and marked it with red paint. It was "struck" by a woman of sacred designation and cut down by her helpers. The tree was shorn of most of its branches, consecrated as sacred, and carried to the Sun Dance camp. On the third day it was erected in the enclosure with a bundle of chokecherry brush (the home of the *Wakiŋyaŋ*, "Thunder beings"), sweetgrass, sage, bison hair, and a red cloth banner. Images of a man and a bison were tied to the upper branches, representing the mythological personages *Íya* and *Gnaška* and the attributes of licentiousness and potency.

The participant dancers were expected to embody the qualities of integrity, generosity, bravery, and endurance. Each was required to give gifts and feasts, to rid himself of possessions, and to make extensive offerings to the Powers. The elders gave instruction in tradition. Individuals might be required to fast, to seek visions, to meditate, to control emotion and action, to observe sexual abstention, and to seek solitude, withdrawal, and silence. On the fourth Sun Dance morning the dancer's feet and hands were painted red and he was dressed in a red shirt, otterskin cape, armlets of bison hair, anklets of rabbit skin, and a wreath of sage. The leader of the procession of dancers, carrying a buffalo skull, walked from the sacred lodge to an altar facing the Sun Dance pole. A pipe ceremony was followed by a buffalo dance and the four parts of the Gazing-at-the-Sun Dance— capture, torture, captivity, and escape. The "captor," as if enacting a war deed, pierced the skin over the pectoral muscles or scapulae of each dancer and inserted wooden skewers. These were attached to thongs leading to the Sun Dance pole or to buffalo skulls. The dancer worked to free himself by tearing the skewers through the skin. Prestige was earned in proportion to the violence of this self-torture.

The Sun Dances I observed between 1967 and 1972 preserved some of the traditional form. There was still the festive atmosphere and a large campground, filled with visitors and returning tribal members. The celebration was sponsored and financially supported by the Tribal Council and was held at the permanent grounds east of Pine Ridge town. Baseball games, a rodeo, and a small carnival were sometimes held during the same weekend in August selected as suitable for a three- or four-day affair. Feasting was still important, with commercial stands and a free public meal of buffalo or beef. Visiting and singing went on around the clock.

The religious part of the Sun Dance during that period was significantly subdued. The pole was sought, marked, cut, decorated, and erected much as in the old way. The selection of the participant attendants had become casual, and the principal shaman mentor worked on a fee contract for the Tribal Council. The candidates, or dancers, were volunteers. Some received day-labor pay. Their preparation began the first ritual day with some instruction from the "Chief Medicine Man" and a sweat lodge ceremony. Gazing-at-the-Sun dancing took place from about 8:30 A.M. to 11:00 A.M. on one or more of the four (or three) days, with piercing on the last day. The participants fasted only during active dance periods and refreshed themselves with sandwiches, canned pop, and cigarettes during frequent intermissions. Piercing was done by the Chief Sun Dancer, who used a sharpened screwdriver and chokecherry skewers about four inches long. The capture aspect was no longer discernible. Instead, the candidates reclined in turn on a blanket. After tearing loose from the thongs, the participants formed a reception line where viewers could inspect their wounds, shake their hands, receive a blessing from the Chief Dancer, and make a monetary donation.

Some individuals with political ambitions saw participation in the Sun Dance (usually short of piercing) as politically advantageous. It gave an opportunity for their names to be repeated publicly and was tiresomely repeated in later campaign speeches and newspaper articles. Others saw participation as preparation for becoming a conducting shaman or as adding to their reputation as a medicine man, ritualist, or healer.

Intermissions at the Sun Dance, especially when a good crowd

54

was present, were adorned with speeches. Some were political, others were set pieces to display traditional oratorical magnificence. Some speakers gave extended commentaries on healing. On one occasion Fools Crow presented an embarrassed young woman and asked her to speak and to walk about. He then described her as having suffered a total paralysis after an automobile collision. She was given up by the white doctors: "I doctor her, and here she is all well."

Sun Dance Notebook, 1967

All activity in early August swirls around the coming Sun Dance. Red and blue posters announce:

> Oglala Sioux Tribal Sun Dance, Thursday, Friday, Saturday, Sunday. Piercing on Sunday at Sunrise, Sun Dance 'til Noon Each Day. All Cash and Beef Donations Will Be Greatly Accepted By the Sun Dance Committee of the Oglala Sioux Tribe. Narrator and Announcer Mr. Paul Apple. Plenty of good water and campground. Not responsible for accidents. Beauty Contest winner will be crowned Princess of the Sun Dance on Saturday.

Pink handbills advertise:

> Peace Sacrifice—Richard "Buddy" Red Bow will pray for worldwide peace by performing the traditional Sundance worship. Red Bow will pierce his flesh and offer his blood, praying for the safety of American servicemen and a peaceful and speedy end to the war in Viet Nam.
>
> Sam White Bear Post 251 American Legion honors those servicemen who have given their lives in the service of their country and those presently fighting in Viet Nam and extends this invitation to all Service Organizations, Veterans, and Servicemen, to participate along with Sam White Bear Post in honoring this day as a counter action against the "Demonstrations" in New York by some of the Sioux Indians.

A tent city has grown across the hills. There are crowds of out-of-state visitors. Youngsters on horseback cruise at dead gallop among the cars. The Sun Dance arena is encircled by the "bahry" (bowery, from the fresh pine branches), a shade of posts and boughs fending off an intolerable sun. Crews of men are stringing wires for lights and public address speakers. Others put long cloth banners on the center pole. A sweat lodge and medicine tipi stand outside the circle.

Our hesitancy gives us away as newcomers and we are immediately greeted by Edgar Red Cloud, the first of many volunteers to offer explanations and descriptions of the coming activities. Perhaps I detect a wish for outside approval and acceptance and a prearranged promotional plan, but the thoughts are lost in the consistent friendship of the following days and the local willingness to explicate the culture in favorable terms. I am not much of a say-hello-to-everybody type, and it was to their initiative rather than my own that I was involved in long informal talks with Around Him, Brings Him Back, Matt King with his huge grin, Jake Herman, Kills Small, Ross Deon, Charles Lone Dog, and Hogan Red Cloud and his wife.

Deon was of the family of *Hošiwic'ak'i,* "Brings the Message" (a mail carrier of the past century, going on horseback from Rushville to Wounded Knee to Manderson and Pine Ridge village). Hogan, "made-a-relative" of the Red Cloud family, is an urban Indian and an aspiring medicine man. He danced the four days, limping on a swollen foot ("snake bit") in a great bloody bandage. Kills Small agreed with my guess about the hospitality: "Yep. We try to get the council members and the elders down here. We want to meet all the new faces and make everybody feel at home."

First Day: On the first day, we were told, the Sun Dance begins at earliest dawn, so where was everybody? A few of us standing around, shoulders hunched against the cold, agreed it would be a treat to find some coffee. But nobody else was awake. The food stands were silent.

After sunrise a group of older men arrived by automobile and entered the sweat lodge. It was still cold. They moved hurriedly, undressed inside and handed out their clothes. The fire tender began to pass in hot cobbles on a shovel. After a perfunctory few minutes they emerged and dressed. A medicine leader, said Jake Herman beside me, led them into the arena, where they danced in a line, whistles blowing. There were frequent intermissions, each preceded by a pipe ceremony. The cloth-decorated center pole had black, red, yellow, and white cloth hangings, a transverse bundle of chokecherry branches, a painted rawhide buffalo effigy, and a similar human figure holding a large, penislike pipe. There were four small subsidiary altars, each with red and white banners. One of dancers appeared Caucasian, maybe wearing a wig with long braids. The alternating dances and rest interludes seemed to me to take on an air of tiredness and disinterest. At 10:30 A.M. the dancers dispersed unceremoniously and the "sacred part" was said to be over for the day.

Edgar Red Cloud had been looking for us—not a long job because the crowd of onlookers was small. He had a handful of pages of Indian stories that were, at the beginning, an account of Iktomi ("Spider," the Trickster). He wanted to explain more about what had gone on in the arena, where he had been a pipe holder, and to invite us to stay in his tipi. Our camp at Three Moccasin was shady and quiet, but we made the move at the loss of comfort and a gain in heat and dust, and great gain in an observation position.

By the time we brought up our gear the afternoon powwow was beginning. First a few, then denser crowds of people filled the shade and promenade surrounding it. The food and soft drink stands were now clogged with people. The drummers began, first the Sioux Travelers and eventually the Porcupines, Oglala Juniors, Roadside Singers, Eagle Butte, and a half-dozen other groups. Dancers trickled in, then flooded the ground. From midday to midnight and beyond, the drums and dancing continued, an ocean of sound, an ocean of intricately costumed performers, an impressive and even ominous spectacle, comparable to nothing else on the continent. During brief pauses the announcer shared local humor and opinion, conservative, pro–

Vietnam war, patriotic. This was the time when the counterculture and black civil rights violence were criticized in the West with great hostility: "You funny-looking people, here is an announcement. There is a barber shop uptown where you can get haircut and show the Oglala people if you are male or female."

Two young whites tried to speak on civil rights but were booed into silence. The announcer quipped: "Those Oglalas in New York. The newspaper said they was in a civil rights meeting. They thought they were going to a powwow. Some people will go anywhere for a free bus ride!" Again and again there was a bantering racial theme, derogatory in varying degrees, against whites (treaty violators), blacks (no respect for law, vandalism), and Indians—"You country blankets don't know your braids from your backsides!"

Abruptly, the announcer called for the dancers:

"Intertribal! Intertribal! What's the matter with you! *Kikta po! Wacʻi po! Wacʻi po!* Let's go!" ("Wake up! Dance! Dance!")

"Here is a lost item! A ten-dollar bill has been turned in. If the owner can identify it he can have it."

"They say the only good Indian is a dead Indian. That can't be so because I see Bob ——— wandering around in here. He's no good and he's still alive!"

"Let's hear from the Wakpamni Singers. They've got a three-dollar donation here from the people from Alaska."

In midafternoon came a pause for speeches, mostly in Lakota, orotund, sonorous, repetitive. Phrases in English gave a hint of the text: "jurisdictional fight," "senators and governors," "the verbal uprising," "Bill 108," "peace," "pride in our boys." Young men in military uniforms were introduced and honoring songs were called for them and others overseas. Peace was a reiterated theme, yet war was important, too. A militaristic culture still?

The announcer continued to punctuate the solemnity with jokes, this one probably aimed at a brother-in-law: "John ———! Go back to your car. Your wife found a woman's purse and some unmentionables."

The afternoon dancing had been preceded by a lengthy quasi-military ceremony. Big-bellied veterans in cowboy boots, dungarees, western shirts, and caps marked "American Legion" and "Veterans of Foreign Wars" marched, lined up this way, lined up that way, led the flag raising and pledge of allegiance, fired rifle salutes, and held hands over hearts during awkward pauses. Both the American and the Sioux Nation flags were honored with speeches about symbolism. After a bugle solo the veterans joined in the dancing, with rifles at trail. Much of this dignified, evidently valued but poorly rehearsed activity was repeated in the late afternoon. It was popular with small boys who raced in to wrestle for cartridge cases, caring nothing for the gravity of the occasion. The public announcer inveighed bitterly against the civil uproars in the eastern cities, emphasized the patriotism of the Oglalas, and condemned hippies. After the Sioux anthem ("All stand! All salute!") was sung, he added a low-voiced coda—"The Red Cloud Treaty said we could fight anybody but the Americans."

On the hillside a man and a woman were cooking over a pit fire in front of a tattered gray wall tent. "Come back and I'll give you a plate of punch." "What's punch?" "Well, it's really paunch. We used to call it pot, or stockyards." After half a day of boiling, beef-gut stew does have a recognizable odor of stockyards. The hand-size hunks of rubbery bowel, flint-hard field corn on the cob (hours of boiling to soften the kernels), and t'ípsila, dried peeled prairie turnips, make a "punch" that appeals to feeders with indefatigable jaw muscles.

The after-supper crowd was dense, overflowing. Outside the circular arbor runs a greater circle, this one composed of food and drink booths—tacos, fry bread, t'aniġa (paunch), coffee. Between the circles is a sauntering mass of the see-and-be-seen, linked-arm girls in shawls giggling at linked-arm boys in cowboy finery, kids underfoot, yelling vendors—a northern version of the Latin paseo.

In midevening the count of dancers passes five hundred. Great swaying, crouching, surging masses of figures, incessant singing and drumming, a go-on-forever rhythm. It produces a feeling of entrainment, as if all were pulsing simultaneously somewhere in brain or soul or autonomic nerves. The dancing crowd began to protest intermissions, to insist that the songs be continued, shrilling with bone whistles that drummers go on and on. The excitement grew infectious and mounted to include the audience. Women ordinarily sitting placidly on the periphery joined in with stiff rhythmic jumping around the drummers, their voices climbing to incredible high wailing crescendos. It was, after a long time, too vehement to be maintained. Some sat on the ground exhausted. Others broke away into the darkness.

The announcer had been silent for an hour and now returned:

"Alfonso ———, go back to the tent. You've got a sick child."

"Bob ———! Bob ———! Get back to your car. One of your wives wants to go home."

"Remember everybody. Tomorrow Senator ——— will speak. Be sure to be here."

At midnight the dancers refused to stop, even when the lights were turned off and the public address system was silenced. Supported, horizontally, by many hands, the drums moved slowly, still thundering, out of the enclosure and up the road, surrounded by an ecstatic dancing throng. I was struggling to tape record this impossible-to-record madness, but was urged sternly, "Dance!" Dance I did, we did, far up the road in the quarter-moonlight.

It is hard to sleep at the Sun Dance, hard to wind down, hard to sit quietly after thirteen hours of crushing noise. Always, somewhere, a drum is going or a song. Suddenly there is a gang fight, or a tent on fire. Or visitors come by with a brandy bottle. Dawn is a long time coming, and the second-day Sun Dance really does begin at first light.

Second Day: On the second day the dancers gathered in predawn light at the medicine lodge. By sunrise they were dressed in long skirtlike robes, feet and torsos bare, listening to instructions from the leader. With the first sun rays they moved in procession

to the arena, always shepherded by the Chief Sun Dancer, for a series of Gazing-at-the-Sun dances, pipe ceremonies, and extended rests. The crowd was thin and a desultory tone seemed to pervade the place. People stayed on the hillside and visited among the tents, perhaps because the western half of the sky was building toward a storm. At noon long lines formed for a free meal—buffalo meat boiled in a huge galvanized vat, wieners and carrots in another, served with bread and crackers and Kool-Aid.

By then the blacker clouds had moved away to the east after a spatter of rain and a tremendous rainbow. Despite the urgings on the public address horn, people drifted in but slowly, enervated by the increasing heat, clinging to tents and shade, not ready for exertion. It was midafternoon before the arena began to fill. Eventually 270 ornately bedizened performers were sedately circling, the men counterclockwise on the outside, the women clockwise near the center pole or the drummers. Children danced in groups or quite alone, enraptured by the music. "Let's have applause for the singers and dancers!"

A pause was called in the late afternoon for the judging of a beauty contest. It turned into a tediously prolonged procedure, won by a Shoshone girl in heavy-rimmed glasses. The announcer, as excluded from the business as the crowd, kept saying, "Let's get this over with!" and "Just be patient a little more, folks!" The after-supper crowd was dense inside and outside the bowery, and at midnight, intoxicated by the many hours of song, drumming, incessant whistling, and jingling bells, it began to insist the drum groups continue without pause. Very much later the entire packed and circling crowd danced out through the wide east gate, carrying the drums and keeping the step. In the center were four utterly transported women in blue and red shawls, a *heyok'a,* and a warrior in a white buffalo-horned headdress. Around them swirled a great clot of ecstatic people, some in costume, some in remnants of costume, many in street clothes.

Third Day: The Sun Dancers, eleven men and five women, file in with the sunrise. Bad Cob is in the lead, carrying a buffalo skull splashed with red paint. The eye sockets and nostrils are stuffed

with grass. This is the piercing day, and many officials jam the announcer's booth. Fools Crow leads the participants through a series of Gazing-at-the-Sun dances, one in each quadrant of the arena. The pipe ceremonies before and after each intermission now have five medicine men, not previously present, who serve as pipe holders. At midmorning the candidates for piercing are formed into a smaller line, in front of the others, all dancing steadily and blowing eagle-bone whistles. One by one they are led from the line, still dancing like hypnotic automatons, and placed on a robe near the Sun Dance pole. Fools Crow pierces the skin over the breast with a sharp knife and passes a wood skewer through the two wounds. A rope, tied high on the pole at one end, is attached to the skewer and the candidate is led back to the line, where he continues his steps in time with the others, placing more and more tension on the rope and his own freely bleeding tissues, the skin stretching more and more. None flinch or fall, and in a half-hour all but one of the eight have broken free. This one, deeply pierced at his own wish, now runs backward at full tilt, breaking the skin, tumbling violently onto the dusty ground. He recovers his footing, joining the others still dancing to the drums. After a closing period of dance and a final prayer, all the participants and dignitaries form a receiving line where hundreds of crowding spectators can exchange a few words and view the wounds more closely. At one end a robe on the ground collects the money gifts.

After the piercing and the reception line the sacred part of the Sun Dance had been completed. To take advantage of the dense crowd a Mass was hurriedly organized inside the Sun Dance enclosure. The altar was a wooden table covered with a star quilt. The ground was littered with waste paper and garbage. The homily contended that both the pipe and the Catholic religion are Christian. "The correct solution is to see that both the pipe and the Sioux Religion came before" ("adumbrated," said the priest). "The same God inspired both. The Buffalo Woman came before Mary and therefore the Sioux Religion should be seen as an early and imperfect inspiration for the Catholic Church. When two pipes are held together like this to form a cross they are also the Four Directions." The homily, continued for what seemed like a very long time, was followed by communion. Edgar Red Cloud and two other men wavered through the hymns, their voices faint but persisting. There was no assistance from the congregation. "Confessions will be heard in a car outside."

Impatiently upon the end of the Mass came a Mormon service, aggressively proselytizing. The young men conducting, in white shirts, dark suits, and neckties, had been conspicuous throughout the Sun Dance days, picking up trash, emptying garbage cans, officiously keeping the back gate, which didn't need keeping. They had put on an execrable Hawaiian music program during the afternoon intermission.

The Mormons seem barely tolerated by the Lakotas and from time to time are expelled from the reservation. They are said to have arranged for many adoptions of abandoned children, "but they interfere too much all the time."

Sun Dance Notebook, 1971

July 29, 1971, P.M., Wounded Knee: The police were busy arresting Bill Schweigman and a large group with him "for having an illegal Sun Dance." Clyde Gildersleeve and Ben White Face, in the spectator crowd, filled us in on the happenings. It appears that Hobart Keith, tribal judge, had issued an injunction against promoting a Sun Dance here, and has now provided a sheaf of John Doe warrants "for all participants, onlookers, and campers." We departed on the run just ahead of the police sweep. Word was that an alternative dance would be held at Wakpamni Lakes the following day. We went, but there was no dance, Sun or other. (Later we learned that the Sun Dance had been moved to Crow Dog's, at Rosebud Reservation.)

August 1: Visited Peter Catches for a long talk and later moved our camp near his cabin. At dawn he conducted a sunrise wedding for an Oglala girl from a traditional family and her Ute groom. Two elder men gave long speeches in Lakota. The bride had seen a draft article of mine on *heyok'a* and felt I did not distinguish clearly enough between rowdy clowns, even if they were masked and of unknown identity, and true ritual *heyok'a*. Her uncle, whose name she would not disclose, was a true *heyok'a*. Her two grandfathers, attending the wedding but speaking no English, confirmed her views as she translated. The wedding feast was *t'aniġa, wójapi* (a kind of pudding made of berries thickened with flour), coffee, and store-bought cake.

It is not yet announced who the Chief Sun Dancer will be.

August 4, Pine Ridge: Late afternoon. A young woman with an ax makes four gesture cuts on a tree near the road. There was no preceding or following ceremony. The tree was cut down, loaded on a truck, and dumped on the ground at the enclosure in Pine Ridge. An hour later it was erected by a crew of men, again without ceremony. A supervisory medicine man had not yet been appointed.

August 5: Sun Dance begins on a cool, sunny morning. Silas Stands, Edgar Red Cloud, and a few others supervise the dressing of the pole, *c'aŋwak'aŋ*, with cloth banners. Eleven venerable men and four women are instructed by Fools Crow and led in procession by Tom Bad Cob, without sweat lodge or other ritual. They include Eagle Elk, Buddy Red Bow, Tyron Apple, a "professor from Colorado" (Caucasian), Russell Means, George Swift Bird, Eddy McGaa, and Hogan Red Cloud. Much of the ritual seems worked out on the spot. There are awkward pauses from time to time.

Reclining in the shade, Peter Catches impassively confirmed that he had expected to conduct this Sun Dance but Fools Crow had been appointed instead at the last moment. He himself is an observer and will not take part.

> This is a *hóc'oka*. A *hóc'oka* is any ceremony. Just putting the tents in a circle is a *hóc'oka*. When you were at my place last year, that was *Waŋbli hóc'oka*, Eagle power ceremony. *Haŋhepi hóc'oka,* that's a night sing, like I told you. *Hóc'okata,* that's the arbor we are sitting under.

66

During the morning pause, a rest in the shade for everybody, the "fasting" Sun Dancers have cigarettes and sliced watermelon: "But I can't wait to go to eat lunch. I'm really hungry."

August 6: It is damn hot and the flies are bad. The tents and tipis have their skirts up to catch the breeze. Dance bustles and head-dresses jitter and tremble on the tent poles, getting fluffed out to wear tonight. We visit with Jealous of Him and Zona Fills the Pipe. Mrs. Frances Coutier says she will send me a photograph of Spotted Crow, a renowned ritual leader. She introduced me to Zona Afraid of Horses, a fragile-appearing matriarch who is one of the marvellously high-pitch singers in the evening celebrations.

At a hand game ("Put your money on the buffalo robe!"), amid much laughter and noise, we talk to Pawnee Leggins, a relative of Sitting Bull; Clifford Pourier, a descendant of Big Bat Pourier; Good Iron; and Vincent Chips, from a family of *yuwipi* and finding-men. Somebody eager for excitement proposes, "Let's go up to the Crow Reservation and ride some of our horses!"

My notebook shows me that we have recorded more than twenty hours of music and song. There is no way I can devise to get at the *fantasy* experience of the powwow dancers during the moments of great transport. Nor of the Sun Dancers. There is no language for either the questioner or the answerer.

August 7: Today thirteen men and eleven women dance. Most are in their sixties and seventies; it is no longer a young warrior's game (a change during reservation times). Four give flesh offerings. Here the dancer sits on a blanket in the shade. The medicine man lifts a point of skin on the shoulder with the point of a heavy needle and cuts it off at the base with a razor blade, leaving a circular wound 2 mm. or so in diameter and freely bleeding. A row of fifty of these from shoulder to elbow and the bloody toweling are displayed as the dancer resumes his place in the line of dancers. The blood spatters and dries in the hot sunshine. The cuts I examine do not penetrate the dermis and heal to form a neat line of white scars. Some ritualists have many overlapping rows of scars, dating to different years.

Broken Rope from Kyle has *c'aŋli icahiye* for sale, and Joe Renville from Sisseton has kinnikinnick and sweet flag root (*Acorus calamus*).

In the afternoon a *wiŋkte,* berdache, is pointed out. He wears a woman's dress over a man's work clothes, a shawl, and a hair net. He is said, by Edgar Red Cloud, to live with a sister. He is about sixty years old, "doesn't work, never did. He always dances with the women. He often carries a white woman's purse" (but doesn't today). A number of girls "mostly from Eagle Butte" dress in male dance costumes and dance with the men.

Holy Dance, at my elbow, said:

> *Wiŋkte* is a freak, a morphodite. One died two years ago. Another one from here is still living in Denver. He was born that way. One man has a lot of horses. They were all freaks of some kind. He wanted to make a show but the law stopped him. They say it wasn't inbred or nothing. *Wiŋkte.* Us Indians have a lot of fun over that. They don't associate with that. Somebody like that is ashamed of himself.
>
> No, I never heard the word "berdache." Sounds like a Mandan word. Or Winnebago.
>
> A woman can have a boy or a girl, whichever they want. They go to a *yuwipi.* Make a little arrow with tobacco on it, a ceremony wishing to have a boy. Or a circle of tobacco knots and a girl's hair tied on it, you will have a girl. The *wiŋkte* comes off on a deal like that—they don't finish the ceremony. As punishment to the mother, to be ashamed of. I don't know if I was right, but I have seen a woman change into a man and a man turned into a woman.

August 8, Hot, dusty morning: Eighteen men and seventeen women begin the dancing. Some others came into the dance area for extended periods (not as dancers), including a Catholic priest from the mission and "helpers" who supported some of the pierced individuals. Two Red Power leaders stood together, raising clenched fists at intervals, seeming to take over the ceremony. In midmorning, speeches of an angry quarreling tone were given by McGaa and Hobart Keith. Keith stridently called the priest "a liar," but without explanation (or rebuttal). Peter Catches, in the audience on previous days, danced today and was pierced with twelve others. The atmosphere was heavy with controversy.

The announcer breaks into the noise with an urgent message: "There will be a meeting of the Little Bighorn Veterans' Association. Remember what the general said—'Let's win this war and get to hell out!'"

This Sun Dance is marked by much larger crowds than in previous years. There are more white tourists, several film crews, and the conspicuous hostility of roving bands of young people with much older AIM leaders. There are no food stands and no running water. A giveaway ceremony was closely patrolled and guarded and the announcer called up people by name to receive blankets, quilts, yard goods, and a large leather robe covered with beading.

In a dance pause a film crew sets up to record a pipe ceremony in the announcer's stand. A Hollywood Western star in stage buckskins and four war-bonneted chiefs go through some of motions dictated by the camera director. "Poking the pice of peep," said Owen Little Bear.

Three different *heyok'a* have made their brief appearances in the afternoons and evenings. They are supposedly anonymous; still, voices in the pressing crowd called out their names: "There's ——— ! That's ——— !"

The Modern Sun Dance

A not-infrequently-voiced Oglala opinion holds that the Sun Dance has deteriorated since the mid-1800s. Jake Herman says, "They do only a small fraction of it." Horn Cloud, who is well read, contends that the Arapahoes and Shoshones at Wind River have more traditional Sun Dances that "go on continuously for three days and three nights." Levi Mesteth thought "the full bloods do the Sun Dancing, the half-bloods promote it, the young people are half-ashamed of it, like it's a throwback to what they are trying to get away from."

The newspaper of the American Indian Leadership Council in 1970 ran an article decrying the desecration by commercialism and the rude intrusions by Christian denominations. Shirley Apple saw the deterioration in other terms—that the people have lost a sense of genuineness, especially in costuming. The most authentic dance outfits are made by non-Indians, by the hobbyists, while Indians replace moccasins with color-banded athletic socks and running shoes (sometimes beaded), use bathing trunks in place of breechcloth and apron, and make dance bustles with nonindigenous pheasant plumes. Of course, wraparound dark glasses and wrist watches are always popular dance dress items. And a flashlight can be handy.

Not a single Oglala could explain some of the segments of the ceremony that puzzled me. Why was the central pole hunted, found, and struck as if it were an enemy? Why were the dancers "captured" and tortured? Why the emphasis on virginity-purity in the woman who aided in the capture of the pole and in the tedious election of a Sun Dance queen?

4. *Yuwipi* and Other Night Sings

The understanding of *yuwipi* is central to the understanding of the many semi-secret healing procedures of the Sioux. Having said that, it is necessary to resay it more accurately. *Yuwipi* is no secret to the Sioux, but operational information about it is not easy to come by, at least at first. The reserve that surrounds it serves to make it unknown or mysterious to nontribal medical workers. *Yuwipi* embodies syncretistic and revivalistic elements of the Sioux Religion and Pan-Indian movements. Politicians seeking popular support subscribe to it. Christian religious workers and medical groups either express approval of it or try to integrate with it without having much appreciation of its dimensions from the Sioux perspective. The principal and powerful and prominent medicine men use *yuwipi* procedures.

Yuwipi refers essentially to the shaman's supernatural escape from inescapable bondage; to his prayer powers, his flight through space and time, his relationship with spiritual helpers; and to his eventual return bearing wisdom and instruction. Elements of *yuwipi* are circumboreal in distribution. The Eskimo and Siberian tent-shaking ceremonies and flying shamans suggest that the essential traits of *yuwipi* have been practiced in northern hunter populations for millennia. Perhaps it is as much a remnant of the Paleo-Indians as is the Clovis lithic technology. Whether or not its archaic nature can ever be fully demonstrated, in the special terminology of the Oglala Sioux *haŋhepi wicʿohʾaŋ* refers to all nighttime ceremonies, *yuwipi* to the belief system as a whole and to the wrapped and tied healer. Using but transcending conjuring, sleight-of-hand, magic, and many variations in ritual, *yuwipi* healers give authoritative medical advice and general guidance in life's problems. The *yuwipi* ritual powerfully defines and reinforces Indian identity.

Healing meetings are held as often as nightly at the request of petitioners who "bring the (medicine) pipe." If the petitioner and problem are accepted by the healer (*wap'iya*), a place and date are agreed upon and instructions are given for preparatory acts, commonly including prayer, good thought, good behavior, fasting, abstemiousness, preparation of cloth and tobacco offerings, and collection of food for a feast.

The *yuwipi* healer professes a power achieved by dreams, vision seeking (*haŋblec'eya*), purificatory rites (*inipi*), and prayer. The terminologies, rituals, and accounts of famous healers such as Poor Thunder, Wound, Plenty Wolf, Frank Big Road, Horn Chips, Flesh, and Good Lance are given in papers by Wesley R. Hurt, James H. Howard, Stephen E. Feraca, and Eugene Fugle.[1] The *yuwipi* medicine man, like many other healers, emphasizes his personal weakness, insignificance, and humility in comparison with the gods and powers, while practicing a simultaneous attitude of omnipotence and omniscience. Prominent *yuwipi* men during the period of my study at Pine Ridge were Frank Fools Crow, Dave Badger, Bear Nose, Thunder Hawk, Mark Big Road, Plenty Wolf, and Aloysious High Hawk.

Fools Crow: A Yuwipi Healer

Frank Fools Crow is a politically powerful medicine man and sage. He is a *wic'aśa wak'aŋ* ("holy man"). He is a *wap'iya wic'aśa* ("conjurer man"), the *yuwipi wap'iya* ("*yuwipi* conjurer"), and is one of several men who conduct the ritual aspects of the Sun Dance. He is priest, medicine man, and a Chief Sun Dancer. He is also a *p'ejuta wic'aśa* ("medicine man"), a medical practitioner, for his district. In 1968, when I first met him, before his rise to national prominence in conjunction with the American Indian Movement and with the Wounded Knee takeover of 1972, he was, by his reckoning, seventy-six. He was a pleasant, thoughtful, friendly, toothless man, heavy of body, sedate, shrewd, good-natured. His speech moved from subject to subject, sometimes with disjunctures that eventually got closed. Of his powers he said:

> I can find things that are lost or hidden. One man lost a new harness. He looked and looked. He came to me. I took him [after a *yuwipi* ceremony] on horseback where the vision told me. There were two holes in a bank. They had put it in one of the holes and covered it very good with grass. He wanted me to tell who did it but I said, "You have the harness back. Be happy. That's what you wanted. That's what you came to me for. No use to get anybody in trouble. You got the harness back.

He gave two accounts of white men who wanted to test him by hiding money in the yard outside the *yuwipi* house:

> I asked them to hide a lot of money, but they would only use fifty dollars. I found it each time and they were convinced of the power of my visions. One of those white man came back. He was going east and asked if he would have any trouble going home. I found out "no" and he didn't. Two weeks later he wrote in ink that he can't break it [a premonition]. He wrote that in two weeks a man would die. *Mnísapa*! In ink! No one can break it! [prevent it or deny it]. In two weeks President Kennedy was shot. I knew two weeks before that he would die, but I couldn't say his name.

A small metal trunk contained Fools Crow's ritual equipment. There were rawhide thongs for binding his fingers, a rawhide rope and a quilt for binding his body, rattles that the spirits animated during *yuwipi* ceremonies, several small hoops with crossbars decorated with porcupine quillwork and plumes (representing *c'aŋgleška*, the world, the universe, unity), and a large medicine pipe. He described *yuwipi* in great detail but firmly declined allowing the conversation to be tape-recorded. Others

had tried, he said, to record conversations and *yuwipi* ceremonies but the machine was always broken by the attempt. Fools Crow commented:

> It is more important to know that spirits are all around. One gives tobacco and food to the departed spirits of friends and relatives, to the grandfathers who go to Heaven with Jesus our Father, to the grandmothers who lay in the ground until they are remarried in the future. I can communicate with spirits and can tell what they say. [During the *yuwipi* ceremony] we may have much crying for the departed people of the family.

Additional ritual equipment included a drum twenty inches in diameter with one head, "speaking stones" (*íŋyaŋ wak'aŋ* or *t'uŋk'aŋ*), and a braid of dried sweetgrass (*Hierochloe odorata*) "to burn and smoke all around the room" to purify the altar and the participants. He described dramatically the tight and painful binding of his fingers, hands, and body; being covered with a blanket; the flickering of the lights; the gourds and drums sounding all around the room. He said if we wished to return sometime, to bring red, yellow, black, and white cloth, and 405 cloth-wrapped tobacco offerings, the *c'aŋli wápahta,* one for each attending spirit. He added, "Try to get Horn Cloud to come as a singer, and if you could arrange that and bring tobacco and groceries, a ceremony could be held. Perhaps."

Of his visions Fools Crow said:

> I am 76 years old. Last year in June I fasted four days on Bear Butte. I see a lot of soldiers, and six bombs in the United States. I saw three crosses at the Sun Dance and everybody glad and holy. Did you hear that whistle at the top [of the Sun Dance pole]? It blows by itself and the man and buffalo move on the Sun Dance pole.

Fools Crow described his veterinary and medical practice as a continuum:

> I doctored horses with sleeping sickness when the epidemic was here. I boiled this root, a *p'ejuta* [medicine] root, and

painted a red stripe from the nose to the tail. They [the horses] groaned. They all got up and were well. I was offered five hundred dollars for it by some ranchers. Doctors pester me to get it [to treat human paralyses]. I cured paralysis in nine horses that way. People, too.

Fools Crow's powers and his confidence in them were strongly demonstrated in his anecdotes: "Emil ———'s boy had diabetes. The [medical] doctors said he would die in twenty-two days. Emil was crying when I met him. I said I would try to give him twenty-two years more. He said he is too poor [to pay]. I say pay me in twenty-two years if I'm right, but they go to the doctors and the boy died in twenty-two days."

Avoidance of claims to omnipotence was not one of his failings: "There was a sick woman. Water came from her nose. Lots of water. She cannot swallow it all and it comes from her nose. The husband said, 'Can you doctor?' He fill the pipe and give it to me. I gave her the medicine and she got well in five minutes." The diagnosis in Western medical terms remained obscure and the medicine a secret.

Another anecdote presented his theory of causality: "I want to try to doctor tumor in the head. Yes, brain tumor. It is bad. It is from a white worm with a red head. It makes a nest in the head, like a boil. When the worm moves they [the patients] are blind and crazy. When the worm moves he [the patient] loses his mind. When the worm is quiet he is all right. I think I could kill the worm and pull it out."

An emergency treatment pitted magic against surgery:

Forty years ago I went to Rosebud. There was a girl working with sewing. She swallowed the needle. It was crosswise in her throat. Six [white] doctors come to the tent there, but they can't get it out. An old man had a pipe. He said "Hokahé!" [a cry of encouragement!] and she got well before sunset. He got a stone and said to her she get well. He breathed [imitating hoarse breathing] and put a stone in her mouth. There was a rawhide all the way across the tent. The half [of] the needle went there when he stamped and shout. Then he did it again. The rawhide shook and he had the other half of the needle. He gave her water and a little grease. They offered him five hundred dollars for curing her but he only took fifty.

Paralysis, contractures, and diabetes call for "hot" foods in prevention and treatment:

White doctors are good, but they can't fix paralysis. They stay like this [demonstrating contractures using his own limbs]. I rub on hot stuff and they get well. They say p'ilamaya, "thanks." The Indians eat hot stuff, kiddin [kidney] and liver. That prevents diabetes. There is a blind man over there. He is thirty and had diabetes blindness. I want to treat that kind of person. You get liver and put it in a saucer. Put on salt. It gets the bad stuff to pass on. Eat it raw. I never use beer, or wine, or whiskey. You eat liver or kiddin and you never get drunk.

Family histories are important to the Oglalas, and Fools Crow validated his own ritual authority by telling of his lineage:

My grandfather, he was Knife Chief, was in the Custer war. He was forty-two years old. He was shot through his right elbow and the chest with a .45–.90 and [the bullet] came out the left [side]. In four days he got well. My father was Jim Fools Crow. Knife Chief gave a Sun Dance because he got well and my father gave the Sun Dance when his father died. That's why I give them.

I can communicate with spirits through the stones. There are flying drums and lights at the yuwipi. The people at Sun Dance are full of praying to God. There are no drugs. They have no food for four days, or water. I give them a cigarette to smoke when they are resting. I give them a little water and dry meat before the first day of the Sun Dance.

Over the years several attempts have been made to integrate Fools Crow's practice with the Public Health Hospital in Pine

Ridge. These foundered on one technicality or another: "Some lady from New Mexico, a community organizer with the Public Health Service, she called me to the hospital. She want me to treat the old people who are homesick there. But they wouldn't give me a house and pay [equivalent to white physicians'] so I didn't go." On another occasion, in an effort to reduce hospital discharges "against medical advice," the Public Health Service approached Fools Crow. No civil service job description could be devised except "orderly." This he refused, because it would have put him in glaring subordination to "beginning doctors."

Fools Crow was invited in 1969 to be a panelist for a two-day federally sponsored seminar on health services. He was an enthusiastic participant and gave two extended lectures in Lakota, pausing gracefully from time to time for his interpreter to keep pace. He dwelt strongly on Oglala tradition and character. The day before the meetings began he was interviewed by three Public Health physicians, myself included. His style of interweaving topics is well exemplified in the ensuing notes:

I can cure gallstones, arthritis, and paralysis in old people. The doctors here can't always do that. I want to treat a stomach cancer. It is a sore inside. My medicine can draw it out. Then the doctors can cut it off or put medicine on it. Then they will be all right. There are bad people, jealous people, who can shoot medicine into people and make them sick or crazy. One man, over at Manderson, was a very good dancer. He won a dance contest and then he fell down right there. He was so tired for a long time, for weeks, that he could do nothing. I found out there was a piece of paper shot into his leg [by a jealous person]. I took it out, and he was well. It was not so you could see it.

He was asked about possible successors: "There are no new medicine men, no young ones. The Navajos are trying to get a school for them. I tried to give *yuwipi* to my [foster] son but he couldn't make it." The most prestigious healer of his district, he nevertheless had no apprentice or student and he gave no particular concern to the issue of replacement.

Fools Crow was more interested in immediate problems, especially the often bitter cross-purposes of Sioux patients and the federal services:

I was by the hospital one day. Down came a piece of string from a window, right by me. Pretty soon a fellow comes walking along, looking around. He stopped and looked around. Then he walked some more. Pretty soon he took out a paper bag and tied it on the string, and up went the bottle. Those people are not working with the doctors. They are hurting themselves. They need someone at the hospital to work with the people, to help them get well and not hurt themselves.

We tried to formulate with him how *yuwipi* works:

Morgan [an Oglala] came to me with a pipe once. He was going to Germany. He brought a pipe. We smoked and went to pray on the butte, and he came back [from Germany] without any trouble. I am going to the Bear Butte for three days in June. I have to go twelve months without bad thoughts or words or acts, or else I can't go. The *yuwipi* stones talk. They tell me what the illness is, if a person has been shot with something, and what medicine to get. I don't know myself. The stones say. They tell me what [the nature of] the illness is and what to do. Like ghosts. A dead boy or girl may hang around the house, annoying. It is because the ghost wants to say something to them [the parents]. I can do that, and tell the parents what the child wants to say.

He rejected my thought that it might have been the *parent* yearning to hear the dead child again or to say to it some regretfully unsaid thing.

Fools Crow had a lively sense of competitiveness and rarely had a good word for his Oglala colleagues in healing. Naming an equally well known fellow healer, he said, "He is a *p'ejuta* man too, but he is half-crazy." And he was no kindlier in discussing the competencies, as he saw them, of white physicians. Basically, he found them lacking in etiological information, in comprehension in a wide but undefined sense, and in the application of skills learned in long practice on patients. Perhaps professional elitism tends to breed derogation of colleagues. He was particularly vehement about peyotists, since their claims at curing alcoholism were widely credited in the Pine Ridge community: "Peyote! That's horse medicine! They are all crazy. I don't like them. I don't like that peyote. It changes your mind. Don't take any of it!" (A reader of these notes pointed out that the manner in which I put Fools Crow's speech to paper made him seem unduly self-inflating. His living listeners do not receive that impression, so I must emphasize that his style, while reflecting the oratorical coup-counting traditions of the Oglalas, is most agreeably balanced with his own humor, pungency, and eloquence.)

Attending a Yuwipi *Sing*

Our first scheduled *yuwipi* meeting was confirmed by several preliminary visits and many exchanges of messages, and at sundown we arrived at Fools Crow's house on Three Mile Creek. Talk ran on for three hours, but his singers were all at Red Scaffold on the Cheyenne River Reservation and no ceremony could be held. It was sixty miles back to our camp.

Some days later we tried again. We picked up *yuwipi* singer William Horn Cloud and his wife, who lived in a cluster of cabins near Edgar Red Cloud in Pine Ridge. Horn Cloud was sixty-one, a gentle, thoughtful, and slow-talking man. His wife, in a long dress and kerchief, seldom spoke, and then usually to her husband in Lakota. When his thoughtful discourse on a wide spectrum of topics slowed down, she would remind him of something with a few low-spoken words, and he would resume his steady conversation. By the time we had driven 120 miles to and from the meeting very few subjects were left unmentioned. As we passed Wounded Knee, Horn Cloud pointed out the arroyos along which many of Big Foot's Minneconjous had fled from the soldiers' guns. His grandfather had been there, he said, and escaped the massacre. His grandmother's body was found in a sandy blowout still visible from the road. Another relative lies in the common grave at Wounded Knee, and from him the name Horn Cloud derived.

Horn Cloud's comments in general reflect the philosophy of the full-blood group of the western Sioux and the disapproval they feel about cultural changes. His description of the *huŋka* ceremony tells less perhaps about that ritual than about the social disintegration that distressed him:

> There are two singers. An eagle plume is put on the person. It is to affirm that he is loved. An adopted child, for example, had this ceremony. It has corn in it, from an old story of a couple who couldn't have children. They tried everything. They were given a corn to plant and it grew and became their son. Nowadays people don't take time to care for their children. They feed them bottles of cow's milk. Cows are not afraid to die and the kids become not afraid to die. They drive fast, drink hard, and act crazy. They are not loved like a *huŋka* child is. The old people and the old ways are the best.

His discussions of indigenous healing often began with a testimonial:

> We took my aunt to a hospital, very sick. They said that she had gallstones but she was too sick [for them] to help her. She was vomiting all the time. The *yuwipi* man sat with her four nights and then left her a piece of meat. He told her to eat it. She was afraid because she was vomiting and was sick a long time, but she ate it and began to feel better. Next morning she was up and made breakfast for the family. She was fine after that. *Yuwipi* men don't ordinarily use *p'ejuta* medicine. But they may advise about them, to take them or not. Medicine men cannot brag or boast or they will lose their powers. They become recognized [as healers] by their results.

We arrived at Fools Crow's in late afternoon. The frame house sits in a cluster of small cabins. The yard swarms with children

82

and dogs. A creek runs behind the house. A mile away against the sunset sky is a conical hill, the sacred hill, *paha wak'aŋ,* used for fasting and vision seeking. We sat talking through the dusk with the family and another singer, Amos Lone Hill. Fools Crow, sitting apart from the conversation, cut and peeled several chokecherry wands and prepared other paraphernalia for the ceremony to come. At dark we were invited indoors for more talk, played with the small children, looked at albums, discussed pictures on the walls. Women were cooking, making stew from a pile of steaks and preparing fry bread. Eventually we all removed to a large log cabin lit by a kerosene lamp on the floor. Twenty adults were present and many children and infants. The door was locked and the windows covered with canvas or blankets. The floor of heavy planks was cleared by pushing all the furniture against the walls.

In the middle of the room Fools Crow prepared a bed of sage. At each corner a tin can of dirt held a peeled wand, each with a cloth banner: white at the upper left, red at upper right, yellow at bottom left, black at bottom right. A larger wand with three ornate eagle feathers was placed at the upper center. Rattles were laid beside each can and tobacco was sprinkled around the assemblage. At the upper center a can of earth from a gopher hill was poured onto the floor, flattened with the side of the drum, smoothed, and inscribed with the symbols of the *Wakiŋyaŋ* (a jagged line with forked ends) and dots and lines representing stars and planets. On the left of this altar, representing the center of the earth, a pipe was laid. A star quilt and rawhide ropes were placed at the foot. The altar and pallet were encircled by *c'aŋli wápaȟta,* strings of cloth-wrapped tobacco offerings.

Fools Crow removed his clothing except trousers and undershirt and knelt on the sage pallet. At first there was much loud talking, laughing, storytelling, but after a while the talk died down. The children grew quiet. Everyone took seats on chairs or on bedrolls on the floor around the walls of the room, and in silence sprigs of sage were passed around to rub on head and arms. The pipe was filled and passed to the senior woman, who held it through the rest of the evening.

After a long song the light was put out. In total darkness an extended prayer was given in Lakota to the pipe, the spirit stones, and the grandfathers. A long song followed and the light was relit. Fools Crow stood, and an assistant tied his fingers, hands, wrists, and arms behind him. A quilt was wrapped around him, covering and overlapping his head and feet, and was tightly bound with a plaited rawhide rope "with seven knots." He was lifted by two men and lowered face down onto the pallet. He moaned and struggled. The light was again extinguished.

A series of long songs in Lakota, led by the singers and drummers with the others joining in, was accompanied by flickering blue lights (one would say, until corrected, from a cigarette lighter without fluid). Vigorous hammering on the floor and walls, it seemed with a heavy stone, denoted the arrival of spirits. The hammering was violent beneath my chair and beside my feet. Sometimes the whole heavy log house seemed to vibrate with it. Loud groans began and the drum sounds seemed to move about the room and across the ceiling. The *p'ejuta wic'asa* gave cries, short phrases, and muffled groans, all becoming more organized, until finally the chief drummer stopped suddenly and called my name loudly.

"I have been asked [by the spirits] to inquire as to your intentions of having this ceremony done." Startled at being asked for a public statement, I could think of no plausible illness or problem. With a new appointment in mind I said, "I have a new and difficult job to do. I do not know if I can do it well. I would like to know if I can." He put this answer, which I fervently wished had been better prepared, into a lengthy statement in Lakota. More singing followed, with groaning, squeaking, and unidentifiable sounds, and deafening pounding on the floor. I was struck heavily in the face by something fur-covered. Small lights like fireflies crackled and flickered. There were agonized bits of muffled speech. Sudden drafts of air could be felt, said later to have been from the wings of *Wakinyan*. The translator, Horn Cloud, at length said:

There is a man, from where you are from. He thinks he is very important. He will go on a vacation but it isn't an

ordinary vacation. He will not come back. He will go beyond. He will die. Now, you will have to take a personal
view about the job. It is up to you. Make up your mind to
do it and you will do it. They will do all they can to help you
and it will be a success. But it is up to you.

He continued with extended comments on the illnesses of
several people present and advice about a surgical procedure that
one woman was scheduled to have at the hospital.

The lamp was relit to reveal Fools Crow sitting quietly on the
sage bed. The ropes and quilt were piled against the far wall. He
slowly dressed and methodically put away his equipment, then
called me aside, as a sponsor of the ceremony, and took me far
from the house onto the prairie. He prayed in Lakota over some
bits of food, ending with the English words "Have pity; help the
poor soul to lead a good life." He threw the food into the darkness and we returned to the house.

The cloth and tobacco offerings from the altar were burned in
the stove. A feast was served—stewed beef, soup, fry bread, and
coffee. The men chatted in Lakota, as did the women. Most
smoked cigarettes. Children were asleep on the floor or in their
mothers' laps. One ten-year-old in cowboy boots squatted com-
fortably against the wall with a can of coffee and a hand-rolled
cigarette. I went around the room saying something to each
person and after much handshaking the evening was over. It was
long past midnight.

Commentaries on Yuwipi

A Cheyenne woman employed as a government secretary:

They have *yuwipi* up at Lame Deer [on the Northern Cheyenne Reservation in Montana] but they call it something
else. My father didn't believe in it. He laughed at it. But he
lost a string of horses for two or three years. He looked all
over for them. He told a *yuwipi* man he was talking to he
didn't see how he could help. He got up and walked away.
The second time my father saw him, a lot later, he had a
hard time getting to see him. He said, "When you believe I

can find them, come back." The third time, my father went over there time and again and he was always gone. When he did see him he agreed to put on the *yuwipi*. He drew a map on the ground and showed my father where they were. My father said he didn't believe it because he had been riding through there many times before, looking for them. But he said he would go, and they were there, and a lot more. The *yuwipi* man said, "Take them all when you find them. They are all yours. Colts and yearlings and all." And that was true. Almost every mare had a colt.

A Sioux woman employed as a hospital worker:

They took my father to Rapid City three times. They operated three times, looking for cancer, and they couldn't find any. Finally they took him to a *yuwipi* man about three weeks before he died. He said, "Yes, he will die. It is cancer. Don't let them operate on him any more." He saved him from more operations that just gave him more pain and didn't help any.

Jake Herman, an Oglala:

There is lots of *yuwipi* here. It goes on all over. Somebody was doing *yuwipi* in one of those houses over there, but I don't know who it was. There are *yuwipi* men and another type. According to their dreams they are Bear, Weasel, Buffalo. They are good for certain illnesses. They get their power by fasting. They use the *haŋblec'eya*, the day crying, the morning cry to the morning star. They have four poles and four tokens and four winds. *Haŋblec'eya*, that's the early-day crying.

Holy Dance, a Rosebud Sioux:

I went to one *yuwipi*, a man whose father died a year before. The *yuwipi* said, "There is a man on the other side of the door. Shall we let him in or not?" The people said, "Yes, because we are here to be doctored of our ailments." They were singing. He said, "Shine your flashlights," and they did, and sure enough it was his father standing there. I been thinking and thinking and I think it was a hypnotizing deal. One of his brothers got angry and said, "Why did you do it? You should never do that," and them womens they began to cry when they saw them flashlights on him. He must have hypnotized us, done something to make us imagine. But finding a saddle and horse, that was true. I been to many of them things and they are not all alike. They are power of the spirit, though.

All these *yuwipi* [men] have a vision first. That's where I got mine. A *yuwipi* gives a preamble about his vision. I don't do the *yuwipi*. I did it twice but found it was no good. I deal with herbs and medicine. They [herb medicine and *yuwipi*] are two different things. They don't match. They don't work together. For someone who has gone through a little stealing, that's [*yuwipi* is] all right. But he shouldn't handle medicine. Some of them do, but they don't handle the medicine very good, and maybe the other part too. So there's two different deals there.

The *yuwipi* spirits are very small. A good medicine man will have about five hundred of them. If he is not so good, he'll have less. If there is something important he'll get help. It takes about a thousand to bring in a saddle. Once they got the guy [*yuwipi* man] from Slim Buttes. They told the man who was wanting the ceremony they needed more power. They had to sing about eight songs. The saddle was a long way off, I guess. They had about twenty singers and every other man had a drum. You could hear the saddle coming. They lit up the lamp and told him to see if it was his. He examined it and it was his. But they wouldn't tell who had stolen the saddle. The next day he wanted his horse back so they sang a lot of songs. They sang all night that time. They said, "You will go up a valley and see many birds. And under the birds you will find your horse." He went up that hill and there was his horse and it was dead, shot, and all kinds of birds over it. Ha! It was there but it was dead and they never would tell who done it.

Yuwipi and Other Night Sings 87

A good *yuwipi* man, if you go to him, them gourds [the rattles] would come to you and talk right in your ear.

White Left Hand, an Oglala:

Charlie Kills Ree in Manderson is very good. Once a plane was lost in winter. It had a debating team on it. The plane couldn't be found. Many tried, including a *yuwipi*. Finally they had a meeting at Charlie's. He wouldn't talk English to anyone. There was a nun present there who had chronic bad headaches. He hit her on the head with rattles. After the lights were on he asked her, "How do you feel?" She was surprised that he could know about the headaches or know her in the dark. No more headaches. And the next morning two hunters found the plane with the dead children. Joe Whiteface can arrange sings. He lives in Porcupine.

An Oglala woman, describing a relative:

She has been a patient at Mental Hygiene in town and complained she was witched by a *yuwipi* man. She complained of being sick all the time and can't work around the house. She got married and divorced and the baby is with her parents. She remarried and her husband is ill. She did not improve, although she was seen several times by the caseworker and was given medication. She says her husband is responsible. She lives in a log house with her mother, who has heart disease. Her mother is a spotless housekeeper but she [the witched woman] is very dirty and sloppy and her house stinks. The *yuwipi* man put a hex on her, she says. She married into his family and he didn't like her. She firmly believes it. Her mother goes to another *yuwipi,* who works with the church and against the *yuwipi* man who witched her. They say he won't let her go until she kills herself. The health aide is concerned with the problem, and is worried and afraid for her. She says the *yuwipi* man "knows what I do and has a little man six inches high watching me." She is immature, depressed, and inadequate. Her husband thinks she is foolish. Her father is a witch doctor, too. All of her family firmly believe in *yuwipi*. She was at a hospital in 1968 for a suicide attempt. Now she is depressed again. She was always sick when she was growing up. She had TB at age eleven and later had meningitis. She blames her suicide and her difficulty in getting help from the agencies on the *yuwipi* man. The health aide says that [a certain medicine man] did put a curse on her. She asked him to remove the curse but she doesn't know if it was done. She is an impossible patient, very demanding and difficult. Nobody can help her, it looks like.

Cornelius He Does It, describing a relative:

One *yuwipi* man was married and had many children. He deserted them and the family went on ADC [Aid to Dependent Children]. He lived with a woman on another reservation. Now he is back, hanging around. He's irresponsible. He is a full-blood. He doesn't work. If he ever worked I haven't heard of it. He is supposed to be a healer. Another *yuwipi* is a veteran of World War II. He's had much trouble with women. He's not an old-time person. It is superficial, assumed, his knowledge. Maybe he is in the Native American Church. He won't say.

An Oglala woman:

My aunt always goes to Ellis Chips [a *yuwipi* healer], never to a doctor. So does her daughter. She's married to a white man. He got fired from his job driving trucks because of an accident that wasn't his fault. Ellis prayed for him and he got a new job better than the other one, and since then he believes about *yuwipi*.

Horn Chips was a medicine man at Wanblee. He found saddles and a lost child in a snowstorm. She had fallen through into a pond. He drew a circle to show where she was and there the body was. They looked where he said and there she was. They knew it was too late to save her before they went to him but wanted to find the body at least.

Sam Wounded lives at Oglala. About four years ago a

high school girl disappeared. She had been picked up by a football star who tried to rape her, and because she threatened to tell her father he killed her with a hammer. Sam was called upon to find the body and did, or didn't, depending on who is telling the story.

Catch-the-Stone: A Preventive-Medicine Procedure

A white woman lived at a rural crossroads, tending a small grocery and gasoline pump. Isolated from neighbors by scores of miles, she suffered frequent burglaries and visits from exuberant and inebriated passersby who had conceived urgent needs for provisions. Groceries were most easily obtained by kicking in the doors. Fearing for life and limb, she procured from a shaman a spirit stone. This protection, she told me, would awaken her in time of danger with a preemptory rapping on her shoulder. Each time, she successfully protected her small house with a rifle. She felt the amulet was infallible. Even when she was too deeply asleep to be aroused, she said, the guardian spirit would cause her to dream prophetically. When she was awake it would whisper in her ear, describing the coming peril in detail so that she could be prepared. She was pleased to show me the wrapped amulet, but she had been warned that to look at the unwrapped stone would despoil it of all its powers. The medicine had been prepared for her many years before by Frank Fools Crow.

When I had known Fools Crow for more than six years he abruptly invited me to participate in a preventive procedure addressing the problems of the isolated rural patient. We were sitting that hot afternoon in the shade of his cabin, discussing the *yuwipi* healing that he practiced and the methods of other practitioners. He interrupted himself to say: "This woman you met here today, the one who brought the white dog. She is sick. We are going to make a feast for her tonight, a catch-the-stone singing. It will keep you from sickness all of your life. Come back tonight and bring your children."

In the late afternoon we gathered in the yard before his cabin, sitting on chairs or on the dusty ground. As sunset faded into dusk the owls began to hunt in the coulee beyond the corral and the nighthawks dived and zoomed above us. The woman patient sat quietly listening to the desultory conversation amid the long, contemplative silences of the other guests. At full darkness we entered the house and sat on the floor against the walls. The windows and doors were covered with blankets. A kerosene lamp was placed on the floor. A bucket of earth from gopher hills was smoothed out on the floor as an altar. On it the shaman drew, with his finger, furrows of lines and dots. From a small tin trunk he took cloth offerings and hung them upon an upright, red-painted chokecherry wand. Praying over each item, he placed a bowl of water, a ball of rawhide rope, braided sweetgrass, several rawhide rattles, a medicine pipe, and a string of tobacco offerings on the altar. The earth was again smoothed, and a new pattern of wavy lines and figures was drawn upon it. Tobacco was sprinkled over the entire assemblage of objects and prayers were offered to the six directions.

The shaman lighted the sweetgrass and waved its smoke over the altar and over all the people present in the room. He sat before the altar and an assistant put out the lamp. In the absolute darkness rattling noises began. The shaman prayed to the grandfathers, *T'uŋkaśila,* and repeatedly intoned, *"Wak'aŋ T'áŋka, úŋśimala ye, oyate kiŋ nípikte ec'aŋmi,"* "God, be merciful that my people may live." Songs followed, accompanied by drumming, then very loud songs and invocations of the spirit powers. Soon came the answers—low spirit voices, flashes of blue sparks, and shrill shouts. The singing, drumming, and praying continued. Heavy pounding, as if from stones, was heard on the roof and walls and from under the floor planks. Small flashes of bluish light appeared and disappeared. Loud cries, hooting sounds, ventriloquistic noises suggesting pain and combat rose and fell above the loud drums. Rattling, shouts, grunts, shrieks punctuated the constant chanting. Long prayers and long songs in Lakota followed monotonously on one another. The black darkness and stifling heat, the dinning music, and the spirit noises coming from all directions contributed eventually to an involuntary blunting of my attention, perception, and discrimination. My efforts to understand details passed into dreamy resignation.

After hours the tempo of the drum and rattle slowed. The

songs diminished, then stopped. The shaman began to pound on the altar, his invocations referring to *mitakuye oyas'iŋ,* "all my relatives." Another voice, shriller, began to speak, rapid and insistent, with hurried hooting, prayer, sighing, and questioning silences. Then, when a silence persisted long, the lamp was relighted. The shaman poured water on the altar, drank from the bowl of water, and passed it around. He pointed dramatically to the altar, where a small black spirit stone (*yuwipi íŋyaŋ*) had appeared. The smooth, shining, opaque pebble, possibly obsidian, was then wrapped in white buckskin, tied to a necklace-length cord, and presented to me with a muttered prayer.

The woman patient who had asked for the ceremony and had provided the white dog and the other food for the feast was given advice from the spirits in Lakota. The ceremonial feast was served from the outdoor fire—boiled dog, fry bread, a berry pudding (chokecherries pounded and boiled with flour), and coffee. A bowl of water was passed, each person murmuring *"Mitakuye oyas'iŋ"* and sipping of it. The ceremony was over and everyone sat back to rest and smoke. After a half hour, while the pipe was passed in preparation for the long drive home, a car was heard laboring up the rutted road and across the ford of the creek. The cabin was so remote that visitors were unusual. Besides, it was after midnight. The newcomers were excited young Sioux who paused to take part in the circulation of the sacred pipe, then broke into an explanation of why they had come. A companion had drowned in a lake fifteen miles away that evening "at the time the ceremony started." They wanted the shaman's advice on where to search for the body.

The catch-the-stone ceremony is similar to the *yuwipi* ritual, perhaps a derivative of it, although no mention of it as such occurs in the published studies of *yuwipi.* Like *yuwipi,* it is addressed to healing. Like the pipe ceremony, with which its elements are intermingled, it utilizes prayer, song, and spirit advice. The catch-the-stone singing provides the participant with an amulet, a magical stone like the sacred stones used by the *yuwipi* spirits, to protect the wearer against illness and danger. The stones are, or contain, or represent, the spirits. A successful *yuwipi* healer must be able to call upon a large and sometimes variable number of such spirits, and can combine rituals or add shaman assistants to increase their cumulative powers. I was told that if disease or injury threatened I would be awakened in the night by the spirits, small beings an inch or so tall, and would be given appropriate warnings and instructions. Also, I would be able to have powerful and protective dreams.

Eagle Medicine

Basically similar in ritual to *yuwipi* ceremonies, the Eagle ceremony has fewer celebrants. These few enjoy a higher prestige and greater isolation than *yuwipi* practitioners and have a more simply defined origin for their healing skills, the spiritual eagle, red hawk, or red-tailed hawk. Each Eagle power dreamer derives major aspects of his procedure from a mentor, an older dreamer-healer. The Eagle power ceremony has been more truly secret, practiced in more remote cabins, and has differentiated from *yuwipi* only recently. Neither James R. Walker for the early 1900s nor William K. Powers for recent decades describes it.[2] In 1969 there was only one practitioner of Eagle medicine on the Pine Ridge Reservation, a deeply religious man who had been a Catholic catechist before returning to Sioux religious practice.

The *Waŋbli wap'iya,* the Eagle power medicine man, was an eloquent philosopher and an impressive speaker. Of his powers, he said:

The power comes from the Dakota pipe ceremony, which began five hundred years, before the time of Columbus. The pipe and pipe ceremony came from someone's vision in the same way I was offered Eagle power. Eagle power happens each time I am given the pipe.

Once an Eagle power ceremony was being given in the winter in a small cabin. It was severely cold at Bear Butte [in the Black Hills] but fairly warm down on the plains at Calico. Food was prepared awaiting the ceremony. The house was dark and the windows were covered up. The

door was locked and no one left or came in. During the ceremony the spirits came and took the pot of cooking meat out of the house through the sky to Bear Butte. There were people who doubted this. They lit some lights, checked the door, and found it still locked. But the pot, the meat, and the broth were all gone. The Eagle power man summoned the spirits and they returned the pot. At the end of the ceremony the lights were lit and the pot was back in the cabin. The top of the broth was frozen, because it had been so cold at Bear Butte.

For the Eagle power *wap'iya,* Bear Butte was a place for fasting, but not more holy or important than many other places. After a fast, he said,

the pipe is used in the ceremony and is what you pray with, like the Catholic chalice and host. It is used to offer up to *Wak'aŋ T'áŋka.* Young people now are too educated. When people were living with the old religion things were different. Now there is liquor and the expression of life is too quick. There is poverty and poor living conditions. Life is very quick now and there are very few people who still cling to the old religions. It would be helpful to return to the old religions in a new form. It would help the Indian people and give them the sort of spiritual strength they need to be able to move on to a less destructive life without such things as liquor, accidents, and people begging and walking the highways asking for rides. I never beg for rides, and I walk to town [twelve miles]. There is a Great Spirit, and what I want to do is help my fellow man.

On another day he continued his philosophy:

When I rise in the morning the morning star tells me whether or not someone will bring me a pipe. That way I will know [if] I must stay home during the day. Someone, sometime during the day, brings me a pipe filled with kin-nikinnick covered with sage. I take the pipe, and that evening there will be an Eagle power ceremony. Word gets around. The responsibility of the person who brings the pipe and requests the ceremony for whatever purpose is to bring the food. Some cloth must be brought, red, white, green and yellow, about a half a yard each. Eagle power in this way is simpler than *yuwipi* because in *yuwipi* there must be five hundred little tobacco pouches. The ceremony will be conducted with the pipe that person brings. Afterwards a gift is made—goods, money, a blanket, or some such thing. Whatever the person who asks for the ceremony feels it is worth to him.

Arrangements for attending an Eagle power ceremony began in April 1969 and were carried forward through May, June, and July. In August 1970 came confirmation of the ceremony, to be held after the Sun Dance. The *wap'iya* set the date and later sent many messages and instructions about changes in time and place, very possibly to give himself time to be surer of me, but also in part because of his full schedule. We were told to bring cloth of the same colors as the banners placed on the Sun Dance pole— white, black, red, and yellow—and enough food for twenty people: fifteen pounds of boiling beef, five cans of corn, a gallon of canned blackberries, three loaves of bread, a large box of crackers, a pound of coffee, five pounds of sugar, a can of milk, and two packages of tobacco. The meal was to be prepared and brought hot to the ceremony, the beef boiled, the berries thickened with flour into *wójapi*. There was talk of an interpreter, but no specific arrangements for one were made.

The ceremony, after many delays and changes, began at 7:30 P.M. in a house north of Calico owned by members of the *wap'iya's* family. The doors and windows were covered with blankets. It became insufferably hot. People sat on the floor against the walls. There were, in all, eight men, eight women, and four children. Two of the men served as singers, and one of the women as assistant and translator. The *wap'iya* explained that the black cloth, brought as an offering, could not be accepted. "This color is used by *yuwipi* men, not by Eagle power men, who use green instead." Nonetheless, we would proceed.

The *wap'iya* gave instructions on how to carry and present the pipe. Held horizontally with left hand down and right hand up, it is received by the medicine man with both hands grasping the stem near the middle. The carrier walks through the door into the room, turning always to the right around the room, and formally presents the pipe. He then sits at the head of the altar facing the *wap'iya*. "The circle business is Eagle. It is also in the Sun Dance, to always circle, and to always dance, never to walk."

The earthen altar (*mak'akaġapi*) on the floor in the center of the room was bordered by five earth-filled tin cans. One held a tall peeled wand with a bag of tobacco tied to the tip, a bag of tobacco placed on the earth surface, and four small peeled wands, each hung with a red cloth banner into a corner of which a tobacco offering was tied. The other cans each held a peeled wand with a large cloth banner (one red, one white, one green, and one yellow). A pail of water with a dipper, a kerosene lamp, a coil of braided sweetgrass, and decorated eagle feathers lay nearby.

The *wap'iya* began with the explanation that one of the women present would translate the prayers because he was exceedingly tired after the four days of Sun Dance. He added that some aspects of the ceremony to come would not be perfect: "There is no sage. It is very hard to find around here. My chief's pipe is in the Sun Dance hole. And I have no rocks. We heat them to steam everything, to purify everything. And we have no drum for the singers. But we will do what we can."

He knelt, lit the kerosene lamp, and directed that the door (that only source of air and slight coolness) be closed. He opened a case, took out his medicine bag (a beaded amulet usually worn around his neck), and placed it on the altar. He lit the braided sweetgrass and tapped its smoking end on all the appurtenances of the altar and waved it in the six directions. A medicine pipe was filled with pinches of tobacco from a skin pouch and smoked to the six directions, each with a whispered prayer. A longer prayer was followed by a song.

The *wap'iya* then stood, turning with the pipe, singing. The light was put out and he removed his boots, throwing them into a

corner. He gave an oratorical prayer, standing with pipe out-stretched, addressing the *T'uŋkaśila*. The next song was joined by the men and women present. At its end the *wap'iya* explained in reverential tones, as translated into English: "Our friend the Red Hawk was here. This is what he said. He came in pity and in prayer. Red Hawk came, and said it is good to see that half of the people here are white men. If you noticed that, that is good. There is nothing wrong in that, that both are at a singing. Maybe there will be more of this."

After the translation, the *wap'iya* commented extensively in English and thereafter gave his own translations. These included a hope for peace in Vietnam and for the safety of the soldiers there, and hope for the safety of his son who was going back to Vietnam. "Because of the Sun Dance [just finished] there will be big changes, changes in the conditions of the world."

He then asked me to speak. I was ill prepared but said, "This singing is held in thanksgiving for a good Sun Dance, and in the hope that we learn all we can about Eagle power." That seemed to suffice, for the *wap'iya* followed with a long speech about his wish that greater understanding between whites and Indians would follow and that in years to come there would be more such gatherings "together in understanding." Then shifting from or-atorical to dialogue mode, he said:

The Red Hawk, *C'etaŋśala,* said you will have a dream in four days. Your face is painted red. If you have that dream you will know you have the Eagle power. You will be certain then. If you do not dream, there are certain things that interfere. Certain things are prohibited. A woman—I hope you will excuse me—that disease that women have once a month. So watch out for it. Don't associate with women menstruating. Or with anger. Or a third thing that is prohibited would be an evil outside interference.

Being good to everyone. Red Hawk appreciated what you did, helping to find the tree and select the tree and the ceremony of cutting it [I had assisted in the ceremony of preparing the Sun Dance pole]. He is grateful, so he will give you a dream. One half is white and one half is Indian. Some day "the man in the center" [*wahoc'oka*, the center of the world—that is, the *wap'iya* himself] will be able to perform these ceremonies for all. For all. It is the only power for good left to us. Others, like *yuwipi*, are evil power. All Eagle power is good and works for good. This power affects all of us. Now we get healing power from it. The Red Hawk has opened his wings over us. You can put sage on your head for direct power. Eagle power will come. Sage will put you in contact with the spirit, and you will know he is there.

After more prayer and a song the *wap'iya* intoned advice and prophecies about the not-previously-mentioned chronic illness of a mother of one of the participants and about her husband's deafness. He asked, "Is there anything else?" One of the singers then gave a long prayer in a soft voice, then the translator prayed, then another woman, then the translator again. Each was accompanied by earnest *"Hau! Hau!"* given in low, explosive, sympathetic fashion. The *wap'iya* translated each prayer and added his own commentaries.

One woman's prayer was for her husband's health and his hearing. Others gave repeated references to peace and Vietnam. The *wap'iya* then prayed, partly in English, for a white woman present. He alluded carefully to her illness without mentioning it, saying that the Red Hawk should "work medicine on her." He gave thanks for the Sun Dance and a recent fast. The lamp was relit. "This will end with the seven songs," he said, and led us through them. The pipe was lit by the *wap'iya*, smoked, then passed to me and around the circle "sunwise" (to the right). After everyone had smoked, the water bucket was passed. As each drank from the dipper saying *"Mitakuye oyas'iŋ"* he was answered by the next person with *"Hau! Hau!"* The *wap'iya* stood, saying, "Well, we will stop. These singings sometimes go on all night." The door was opened.

With all still seated, dishes were passed around and a young man who was not present during the ceremony dished forth the beef, soup, *wojapi,* bread, crackers, and corn. No one ate until everyone was served, a prayer given, and *"mitakuye oyas'iŋ"* said all around.

The two-hour ceremony was done in a hushed atmosphere and mostly in Lakota, a language well suited to eloquence. The mood of the participants and of "the man in the center" was reverential. "We call it," he said, "a singing." The room was still incredibly hot. I knew my attention had wavered despite desperate efforts to scribble notes in the dark and to miss nothing. A year's wait for this experience had given me a high state of motivation to be attentive, yet I had drowsed at times. Or dreamed.

The Eagle Power Medicine Man

I first met the Eagle power *wap'iya* in April 1969. He lived on a hill near Payabya in a new, well-built cabin with log walls and earth roof. It had served one winter.

He was perhaps sixty. His long hair was tied at the nape with a red ribbon. He was pleasant, reserved, and thoughtful. Later on he became articulate and philosophical. He lived, as he said, "in poverty and in beauty, close to nature." He described the hills and breaks with affection and appreciation. His cabin was just below the rimrock and the pines. The view was magnificent.

He gave a strong impression of devoutness and sincerity. He talked slowly about Indian religion and values, of his respect for and oneness with the country, the grass, the weather. His eloquence reflected his years as a teacher of catechism at the Holy Rosary Mission. "But now I live with the world, with nature, with the grass coming up, everything." He had returned to the Sioux Religion without giving up Catholicism, and had adopted old ways. The long hair, he said, "gives much unfavorable attention but it is my way."

He described Eagle power as a curing ceremony much like *yuwipi* but used it only for curing. It is said to be efficacious in gallbladder disease and tuberculosis. The singing and prayers are similar to those in *yuwipi,* but it is not held in total darkness.

It comes from Crazy Horse by way of Good Lance. *Yuwipi* and Eagle power are similar but different. I got it from Good Lance. It was passed on to me and I am doing it in the exact way.

To conduct a Sun Dance one must have been pierced four times. Fools Crow has never been pierced. His powers come in hereditary ways, from father and grandfather. There are *yuwipi* and Eagle ways of conducting the Sun Dance.

He competed each year, sometimes bitterly, with Fools Crow for the Tribal Council's contract as Chief Sun Dancer. He conducts fasts and goes to Bear Butte in June to fast. He welcomed me to attend a fast or an Eagle power ceremony.

It is all based on the power of the pipe. At a Sun Dance years ago a great storm came. I put up the pipe and the storm divided. There was no storm where we were but there was great damage, I heard, in other places. Houses were blown down, but the storm passed us on both sides.

The experience of the Sun Dance I can't describe. It's like being hypnotized. As I go up and down [dancing] it's as if the sun were dancing. It is a good feeling. It is all preparation, planning, fasting, being ready. It is not easy. My throat is dry and I am tired. I don't sleep before; I cannot sleep. I am thinking and planning how it will be. There is sacrifice, pain, death, and dying, and coming back again to the real world. You can tell if the Sun Dance leader is a real leader. If there is rain or great wind he is not proper for it. The Sun Dance is for the generations coming. For the boys in Vietnam. Someday I want to have a real Sun Dance, at Spring Creek on the Rosebud or in the hills. No metal, no glass, no cars. My first Sun Dance was in the hills, way off there.

He was disdainful of the curtailing of a recent Sun Dance for nonreligious reasons, of the associated commercialism, of the dilution of the serious nature of the Sun Dance when it is held near town, and of the degeneration of the ritual.

He is the father of eight children. He himself was an orphan, reared in poverty. He worked as a laborer, farmer, and cowman and was for five years a catechist at the mission. He considered himself devoutly Catholic, a religious, nonpolitical person. He held himself apart from the towns and the tribal government and organized activities. He wanted the Sun Dance recorded carefully (part of his reason for welcoming me):

> Pictures right in there, the real thing, of the piercing and all, for the other generations. Christ would have wanted it that way. I will do as many Sun Dances as I can. I may die this year, but I will go on. I am prepared to die. I expect to go to Heaven. Jesus will judge me. When I see I am going to die I will fill my pipe and present it to Jesus. If he accepts it, it will be real peace. He may hit me on the head with it, or he may send me to one of the mansions he has prepared for me. I live here in poverty, with nature. I look at the hills and the sky and the grass coming up.

After this first meeting I was many times a guest at his cabin and attended healings, weddings, sings, and pipe and sweat lodge ceremonies there. I assisted him one year in the preparations for the Sun Dance and in other years took some part in that work. In those years he was seriously ill with a duodenal ulcer and gallstones and was repeatedly in the hospital at Pine Ridge and Rapid City. My visits to his home sometimes found him ill in bed, yet he would not move into town where medical care was more easily available, and his trips to clinics often involved miles of walking in winter weather to the highway and along it, for he disdained to hitchhike.

During an intermission in the Sun Dance in 1969 I sat smoking with him in the shade of the arbor when a man came to him with a foot gashed and bloody from treading barefooted on glass. He made a sentence or two of muttered prayer, rubbed his medicine bag on the wound, and dismissed the apparently satisfied patient without bothering to look for imbedded glass or a diminution in the hemorrhage. The medicine bag he made for me, a replica of his own, was alleged also to be a sovereign remedy.

His integrative powers were impressive. He not only retained a working position in the Catholic Church; conducted Sun Dances; and officiated at frequent Eagle pipe ceremonies, sweat bath ceremonies, and weddings,[3] but also, with some uneasiness, I thought, was an officer in the Native American Church.

5. Other Medicines

The medicine power of ceremonies, dances, and societies may derive from sources other than those described for *yuwipi* and the spirit eagle. The vision quest, for example, evokes a wide spectrum of internal experience and tutelary personages. Further, the problems to be dealt with by a practitioner may play a major role in the structuring of his special knowledge and functions. The Bear society, for instance, may have coalesced around teachings of trauma surgery. Syncretistic influences have contributed to the structure of recent practices such as peyotism and faith healing. This chapter considers some more or less distinct entities of medical and magical practice.

The Bear Medicine Society

The bear is a fearsome animal, competing with humans for food and natural shelter, hunted by and predator upon ancient peoples since the Pleistocene. The Neanderthals gave respectful attention to the great cave bear and left behind his ritually arranged skulls and limb bones. The grizzly is an awe-inspiring animal today even in his relict numbers and with the protection of modern weaponry. Confronting him in prehistory must have been the peak experience of the extraordinarily brave or the terminally unlucky. His attributes have been woven into the mythology and protective magic of hunters, and his symbols into religion, combat, and medicine.[1]

In the nineteenth century the Sioux had a Bear society with

membership composed of those vision seekers who had been graced by a supernatural experience, *mat'o ihaŋblapi,* "they dreamed of bears." Bear warriors and bear shamans had distinguishing costumes and behaviors. Among the Assiniboines, close linguistic relatives of the Sioux, for example, Bear society members had distinctive patterns of shirt, hairdress, face paint, knife, shield, and tipi. They developed war groups who specialized in ferocious bear-imitating charges upon the enemy, gave bear-honoring feasts and rituals, frightened their neighbors, and treated the sick. The Teton Sioux Bear society had similar attributes. The dangerousness of Bear society members and the fear they often inspired derived from their imitations of the attacking animal.[2]

Frances Densmore wrote that the bear "is the only animal which is dreamed of as offering to give herbs for the healing of man." James R. Walker's interviews with Lakotas include Red Hawk's assertion: "I am a *wicasa wakan* and I know the *Wacipi Wakan.* I know the *Wakan Iya, Econpi,* and *Lowanpi* [*Wakan* speech, actions, and songs]. . . . I am a medicine man and know the Bear medicine." Walker had data also from Thomas Tyon about the Bear society, with emphasis on the treatment of wounds by ritual and medications, one of which, an aromatic "white medicine" given by inhalation, prevented the festering of wounds.[3]

Walker presents a detailed description of treatment of the sick by a Bear medicine man (*Mat'o wap'iya*). The causes of disease were held to be *wak'aŋ, wak'aŋla,* evil mysteries, poisons, snakes, water creatures, or shamanic powers. The basic healing equipment included drum and rattle and a repertoire of music. Each treatment required its specific song. The ten basic *p'ejuta* (medicaments) were *t'aopi p'ejuta* ("wound medicine"), turtle heart, and tobacco for wounds; cedar to disinfect; yucca pith for swelling; "blue medicine" for anemia; *siŋkpe t'awote,* or calamus, for delirium and diseases of the head; "sweet medicine" for failure of menses; "yellow leaves" for swellings; and yucca powder for stomach pain. The medicine man of this society used a sharp flint to cut around wounds and inflammations. Bear medicine may have been based on experience with the treatment of battle injuries. Wolf society members, also a warrior sodality and distinct from the Bear society, prepared war medicine and were held to be adept at removing arrows.[4]

A brief reference by Lame Deer documents that the Bear society remains within living memory. Stephen E. Feraca thought that Bear doctors were formerly common at Pine Ridge but had been replaced, possibly entirely, by *yuwipi* practitioners.[5] That stood in agreement with my experience in the years 1967–72; no Bear medicine men could be found on the Pine Ridge Reservation and I took the society to be extinct until Joe White Face, a part-time *yuwipi* man at Porcupine Butte, disagreed:

> My grandmother's cousin's husband, her father was a Bear medicine man. Named Wears-a-Bone-Necklace. *Huhu nap'iŋ* [literally, "Bone Necklace"] means really "bear claws." Anyhow, my grandmother's cousin married this Bone Necklace. He went out deer hunting and found a cub bear. On the fourth night the cub sang for his father and mother [saying] that he was suffering. His wife said, "You better turn him loose or something will happen." He took him way out. On the fourth night the cub and the father and mother came to him and said, "I'll give you my power." That's how he got started. Bear medicine men can fix fractures of the arms and legs and also bleeding. They can take care of anybody who has been hurt, like falling or getting shot or cut.

The legendary ferocity of Bear society members is still recalled by the Oglalas. One medicine man believed: "Children and dogs should be tied up when those people are around. I saw a Bear medicine man going along growling. Then his tusks grew, just like that. A dog barked. He jumped and tore the dog's insides out with his teeth. This is an actual story, a real medicine man."

The Horse Dance

Šuŋkwac'i, the Horse Dance ceremony, seems now to be dormant or defunct at the Pine Ridge Reservation although it was performed in recent decades. Black Elk's account is recorded by John G. Neihardt and by Raymond J. DeMallie. Feraca described a Horse Dance at Oglala in the 1940s, given to end a severe drought. Four groups of four horses (a twice-sacred number) were used and rain and hail followed. Feraca himself witnessed a Horse Dance in 1955. Two riders appeared during a Sun Dance, dressed in breechcloth and moccasins, with black hoods over their heads. Their bodies were painted. In the sage circlets around their heads were eagle-down feathers. Four women preceded the dancers into the arena. Each carried a staff and a colored cloth banner and took a position at one of the four cardinal directions. The two riders entered, one offering a pipe to the sun, the other offering a sage circlet. The horses were trotted during the songs, then ridden wildly about and out of the arena. Before they were out of sight it began to rain heavily.[6]

The Horse Dance is related not only to bringing rain but to the cure of mental disease and nightmares. Participants must have had dreams of the ceremony or of dancing horses. Dancers may have the assistance of a medicine man and use the eagle-bone whistles characteristic of the Sun Dancers. The horses are unbridled and are ridden bareback.

Few of the older men who were my informants remembered the Horse Dance songs, but Holy Dance said:

I seen the Horse Dance a long time ago at Manderson. It was just before a war, to bless the horses so they don't get hurt or sick. There were good medicine men then for horses. Like veterinarians. They were good. Their medicine don't work on humans. They were sure good veterinarians. I don't know [even] one herb for that. They could cure distemper in three or four days, all that brains and stuff coming out.

I used to be a good horseman. One horse [I had] seemed locoed. I couldn't ride him or anything. That Indian took something from his pocket and rubbed it again and again on his [the horse's] face. The wind would blow it towards his nostrils. Then he said, "Go ahead" and that horse never moved. He didn't run or bite, but I was afraid. His head was hanging down. After a few minutes he went around gentle, gentle! It [the medicine] was strong. It ruined him. Too much inhaled or something. His [the veterinarian's] name was—he had a lot of names—was Turkey Track Bill, or Henry Buffalo, or Hairy Shirt. I think that's his right name. He was very tough, but in the end he became a preacher. He died last year. The Horse Dance will cure anything mental. Like loco in a horse, or loco in a person. And strokes that bother the mind. A person who is mental should be treated right here with *šuŋkwac'i*. They shouldn't send them to the big hospital [state hospital]. They never come back from there.

Weasel Medicine

North of Calico, where the road turns to cross the White River, is an ancient country store, a lounging spot in winter and summer for people in need of company and conversation. Nailed to the wall above the counter is a weasel bundle, a cased skin stuffed with red cloth and wound about with beads. Its secret medicine contents ensure the health and prosperity of the house. Will the old man sell it? "No, it's been there twenty-eight years. Wouldn't sell it for nothing." Another weasel amulet, this one in a cabin near Potato Creek, was "a protection for the house." It had been made by a Weasel dreamer, his name unremembered, "and nobody makes them any more." Weasel medicine seems to be defunct or at least quiescent. Perhaps it was more nearly an amulet complex than one of the night-sing groups. We found no other information.

Ghost Medicine

Definitions vary or are contradictory concerning the distinctiveness of ghost medicine, *wanaǧi p'ejuta*. William K. Powers did not discuss it. Walker did not differentiate it as a medical system in the early 1900s, although he made extended comment on the *naǧi*, "who are in the world all the time"; the *wic'a naǧi*, the spirit of a human; and the *wanaǧi*, ghost or soul, which leaves the body after death and journeys to the spirit world. Ghost medicine should not be confused with ghost-keeping rituals for the dead nor with the messianic Ghost Dance. Ghost medicine is thought of as one of the many *yuwipi*-like rituals named for the tutelary spirit revealed to the *wicʿaśa wakʿaŋ* in his vision experiences. According to Wesley R. Hurt, ghost medicine doctors used "the power of the pipe" and herbal remedies.[7] Stephen Gay, an Oglala from Porcupine, South Dakota, said:

> Ghost medicine is *wanaǵi pʿejuta*. A *pʿejuta wicʿaśa* is a ghost medicine man. They had great power. Once a group of men were traveling. A party of the enemy was coming over the hill. One said, "Just sit down; they won't see you." The enemy went right through among them, looking around, and did not see them. Or a man singing right there, and you can't see him. There was an old story my father told me. A buffalo was mired in a spring creek, going down and down and making bellowing from underground. *Ohaŋ!* It was a ghost buffalo, under the ground!
>
> Ghosts attack a person and make their mouth or eye droop, so ghost medicine men can help that. Strokes, like that. *Wanaǵi* is a ghost. They can affect your mind and make you crazy. A ghost doctor can fix them strokes.

A white nurse at the Public Health Hospital in 1968 said: "There is a ghost medicine man in Slim Buttes who is much like an Eagle medicine man but gets his power from ghosts. His son was a patient on the surgical service for a long time. He complained of seeing ghosts all the time, and didn't want to see them."

Ghosts are thought to be the special cause of mental illnesses, although some Oglalas condemn peyote, alcohol, and drugs for mental effects. The older and tradition-oriented Oglalas seemed almost unaware of marijuana and hard-drug use but the same was far from true for the younger people. Profound and debilitating alcoholism is a visible and common addiction. Psychoses among adolescents have been ascribed to glue or gasoline sniffing.

I was unable to interview a practicing ghost medicine man to confirm his particular attention to mental disease and addiction. It should be emphasized, however, that *yuwipi* healers address themselves without hesitation to such psychiatric illness. Several individuals carefully denied any knowledge of ghost medicine except to say it was no longer practiced, and then after a pause referred to the ability of the ghost medicine adept to make himself and his companions invisible, especially in war. Invisibility was not mentioned in any other ritual context.

Holy Dance repeatedly expressed an uneasiness about the possibility of being hypnotized from a distance, about being confused or manipulated by an enemy, something other cultures might call black magic. He equated this with ghost medicine, a power called upon in warfare or in witching or hexing.

The Ghost Dance

The millennial religion of 1890 promised to abolish disease and death. The earth was to be refreshed and the white people and all their works would disappear. Dead relatives of the Ghost Dancers would be restored to life. The buffalo and horse herds would return. The Ghost Dance teachings, which spread over much of the West, were derived from autochthonous earth-renewal ideas and from Christian doctrine. From midsummer to midwinter of 1890, the revival occupied increasing numbers of the Sioux. As the excitement grew, off-reservation white communities began to fear that the dancing was a prelude to war and agitated for armed intervention. The missionaries, losing control of the Lakotas' hearts and minds, began to preach that the Messiah wasn't coming after all. At least not yet. And not here. Reservation agents issued prohibitions against dancing and gatherings, which were ignored. So they called for force. The Sioux, apprehensive, ran. They were pursued and the affair was elevated in the press to an "outbreak." The ensuing massacre at Wounded Knee Creek will never be forgotten by the Oglalas nor suitably atoned, but it was not the end of the Ghost Dance religion, which continued to be practiced, surreptitiously and by small numbers of Sioux, who still hoped to see its promises fulfilled. The ceremony lives still in the memory of several of my Lakota friends. One might presume that it is as potentially revivable as was the Sun Dance.

Holy Dance described a Ghost Dance performed in the hills in secret in 1909, the purpose being "to prevent the government taking any more land." And he remembered other Ghost Dances in his childhood, held in the hills, with guards to warn of the approach of police.

He began to demonstrate the Ghost Dance, showing by gestures the dancers holding hands, going back and forth in a surging manner in a circle, then around, men and women together. As he sang and danced he became more and more enthusiastic, then ecstatic.

We got good land,
We must keep it.
That's what my Father said.
While you are living on the land, be good.

Don't hurt your health.
That's what my Father said.
The land will be here forever,
We may not,
So we wish to live a long life.
That's what my Father said.

It's like a poem. It keeps saying, "That's what my Father said."

The death song of the old woman said:

My son was a brave man,
But now you are laying there pitiful,
Laying there pitiful.

The Korea song says:

You boys in Korea,
You should have took your pipes
And prayed to Wakˀaŋ Tˀáŋka
That you would come home alive.

The *huŋka* ceremony is gone. They don't do it any more. The dance and the song is gone. Mostly women did that. And there is no singing of the Horse Dance [i.e., no one remembers the songs]. Nobody knows how to sing it. It's fast, like between the peyote and the *yuwipi,* the beat. It's real fast. But if the young ones remember the Ghost Dance songs they will be all right.

Peyote and the Native American Church

The importation and use of peyote is relatively new to the Northern Plains. Among the Teton Sioux its distribution followed the growth of the Native American Church. Peyote buttons, the entire dried plants of *Lophophora* containing the hallucinogenic mescaline, are a trade item. The plant does not grow north of Texas. Ritual equipment is often imported along with the buttons. Ritual objects in the peyote ceremonies of the Southwest are traded into the Dakotas, Montana, and Canada. The peyote fan is made of the pink and white plumes of the scissortailed flycatcher. The water drum and distinctively beaded gourd peyote rattles do not seem to be in the Teton tradition.

Peyote is called *p'ejuta,* "medicine," by the Oglalas and is considered a sovereign remedy by those who use it. It contains power and can thus overcome illness "in a sacred way." The extent of peyotism of the Pine Ridge Sioux between 1965 and 1973 was not easy to determine. There was a strong emphasis by the peyotists on humility and secrecy, and a prevalent (and perhaps irrational) fear of narcotics informers, even though the sacramental use of peyote by members of the Native American Church is now legally protected. The severe disapproval and contempt of Oglala nonpeyotists stemmed from the belief that the drug produces insanity, laziness, and moral dissolution. Not mentioned, but possibly more important, the Native American Church competes successfully with both Christian churches and traditional religion. Officers of the Tribal Council, herbalists, and *yuwipi* people, most of whom held themselves righteously above the peyote users, provided much anecdotal information. Their

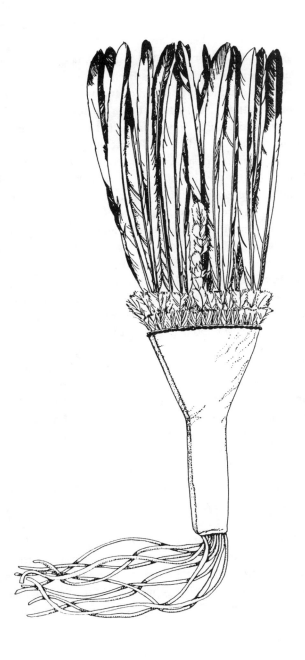

strong dismissive attitudes, however, did not always inspire confidence in the accuracy of their information.

At the Pine Ridge Reservation the Native American Church division called Cross Fire emphasizes Bible readings. The Half-Moon group was conducted in a "more Indian tradition" with meetings held in tipis. Both rituals begin at dusk and extend through the night to daylight or beyond, with drumming, singing, prayers, confession, and meditation. Peyote buttons are chewed, consumed in the form of paste, or taken as a tea from a communal pitcher. Since it is considered a supernatural substance and literally contains *wak'aŋ* attributes, it is taken in four doses, the requisite sacred number. Thirst and nausea follow.

Meetings are conducted by a Road Chief, assisted by Fire Tenders, a Cedar Chief, and others. Strong emphasis is placed on proper personal attitudes, moral behavior, religious faith, deep silent thought, and individual humility. A "water call" held at midnight and at dawn resembles the water ceremony in *yuwipi*. The ceremony ends at dawn with the Peyote Woman's prayer. She is the benign adviser and dependable caretaker. Much of the night is spent staring at the fire ("contemplating Indianness," Edgar Red Cloud said). There are extended talks and testimonials about personal faith, self-discovery, goodness, intentions to improve one's life, and illnesses. Vomiting (induced by the bitter alkaloid) is common. Members carry a vomit cup or can. Vomiting is welcomed and is thought to expel poisons either spiritual or corporeal.

The reiterated purpose of Native American Church meetings is to achieve healing and transcendental insight, self-confidence, strength of mind and body, and happiness. Peyote meetings are considered by devotees to be especially efficacious for alcoholism, nervousness, and insanity. Its opponents say it causes those illnesses. Perhaps a selective process operates to bring persons with alcoholism or overt mental illness to peyote meetings and the group thereby earns its public reputation. Many Sioux go out of their way to emphasize their ignorance and fear of peyotism and say it is foreign to Teton culture and is "against the pipe and against the true Sioux religion." But fairness would suggest that elements of peyote ceremonies are fully consistent with the formalized self-pity of traditional Sioux rites and, most especially, with the vision quest.

Important Oglala peyote leaders in the period 1968–73 were alleged to be Douglas Horse and Silas Grant. An annual tent meeting of the Native American Church was held each June at the town of Kyle with Albert Spider conducting the proceedings. Levi Fast Horse, known as a *yuwipi* man, is also a member of the Native American Church.

Oglala Commentaries on Peyotism

Edgar Red Cloud was a sagacious elder citizen of Pine Ridge. A descendant of the military and political leader whose name he bore, he represented one full-blood attitude toward peyotists: "Don't have anything to do with them people, they are all dangerous and crazy." A Tribal Council member who considered himself "Americanized" was impressed with the therapeutic and constructive potential of peyote: "A man I know had tuberculosis and a bad emotional problem. There didn't seem to be any hope for him. But he joined the peyote religion and now he is okay." A white cattle rancher who considered himself "Indianized" and who depended upon the reservation labor pool, believed: "Peyote is good for drunks. Some guys who never were worth a damn, undependable and dishonest, get in the peyote church and it makes new men of them. They don't get drunk anymore and they are good workers for the first time in their lives."

Few Oglala peyotists will discuss the Native American Church with a nonmember. The ones I knew described a strong influence of meditational and psychedelic philosophies, learning to understand oneself in a transcendental way, and achieving profound personality changes through meditation and drugs. They spoke in the rhetoric of counterculture religions adopted from the white community:

You have a deep change and become well from all illness, mental and physical. The next morning after peyote you feel well and whole. You give up pessimism and despair and see that everything is similar, not different. Problems become joy. You accept everything in the world and give up struggling with external reality. You learn to know yourself and to stop being negative. Peyote can also be used when a person is ill with fever, sores, or an injury, for it cures all disease.

I thought I heard an echo of Tao in one peyotist's phrase: "A good long laugh is the paradise of the peyote people."

One medicine man, a close friend for many years, was ordinarily candid with me, but he refused to talk about peyotism, saying, "I don't go to town much and I don't know nothing about it." He professed fear of peyote users, but when I visited him one autumn there was an ash-filled Half-Moon peyote altar in his yard. His only comment was: "Owing to circumstances beyond our control we are having peyote sings here now." He was himself the Road Chief.

Alcoholics Anonymous

Alcoholism is tragically common on the Pine Ridge Reservation. It is the traditional killing disease of the American Indian and the source of many restrictive laws. Off-reservation bars are popular, especially the ones alleged to encourage the dissipation of Welfare and Aid to Dependent Children checks. The insensate, cyanotic drunk lying on the sidewalk in the hot sun or on the roadways at night, the violence in the bars in Whiteclay, Nebraska, the fistfights and gang fights with drunken whites, the frequent car wrecks, the massively disorganizing addictions of young mothers and of family heads, the rowdyism of adolescents, all contribute to the prejudicial white contempt for "worthless, drunken Indians" and the widespread social and economic sanctions against reservation people. Along with suicide, tuberculosis, and family disintegration, alcoholism is a major unsolved problem of the Sioux.

In 1968 there were three Alcoholics Anonymous groups. One

at Wounded Knee was led by a man who had the reputation of being "semi-mystical and too Indian, but it works!" The meetings included singing, drumming, and prayer. Another AA chapter was called "The Saved-in-Christ." Its leader said his approach was didactic: "You got to get past the primitive thinking. You get him away from his primitive notions and instruct him what to do." However accurate these descriptions of method, too brief to be satisfying, designated healer-leaders using some traditional elements of Sioux religion and Christianity are active in the treatment of alcohol addiction. In yet another Alcoholics Anonymous chapter in Pine Ridge, more conventional AA approaches were used, and both whites and acculturated Sioux attended. Descriptions and efficacy studies are nonexistent.

Fundamentalist Christianity and Faith Healers

A 1969 poster displayed in a country grocery proclaimed "Divine Healers! The Body of Christ Indian Crusade! At Black Feather's place on Wolf Creek 14–16 August." On the fourteenth a few cars and horses collected around a row of ramshackle houses. A few tents went up. The enormous expanse of rolling tall-grass prairie ended in the pine hills on the southern horizon. An empty Sun Dance circle was just visible to the northwest. To the east was the ruin of a long-abandoned dance enclosure. The posts were still up, but the bough-covered shelter was rusty-brown and dead under the summer sun.

Little was happening when we arrived. The day was hot, the sun was fierce, there were no trees, no shade. The still-saddled horses stood head-down and motionless. The dogs crept under the cars and ceased to threaten newcomers. The people visited and ate and slept. There was no drinking. In the evening a brief outdoor service was held. No whites were present other than my two children and me. The sermon was in Lakota. After dark people drifted off toward home.

Like their white counterparts, the rural Sioux enjoy revivals and tent meetings in the good old tradition of the evangelical denominations. In the rhythms and excitement and church music there is perhaps some echo of the traditional Indian dance bowery. In the abandonment of oneself, the relaxation of critical thinking, the emotional embracing of a great powerfulness beyond one's daily life there may be something that urges people to testimonial and commitment. (William Henry is the author of the excellent phrase "The common throng's yearning—in this or any society—for ritual pieties as an alternative to reason.") And there is always an emphasis on the healing of body and soul. To the receptive person the orgiastic experiencing of faith, hope, and trust is to be traded for no other. How can we link this emotional upsurging with the healing effect so stoutly claimed for it? The flooding-in of the Holy Spirit, the fusing of self to divine power, the abdication of rationality and personal control to the epiphany surely makes the congregation "feel different." And maybe different is better.

The holiness-pentecostal movement in Christian churches has had wide acceptance in minority, disadvantaged, and Third World populations. A consideration of its antecedents and the vicissitudes of its acceptance in American Indian reservation life has not yet been attempted, but an examination of historical Sioux religion suggests that the vision quest and its related conceptual structures pre-adapted the Sioux for fundamentalism.

In the eighteenth century the sermons of John Wesley introduced "enthusiastic Christianity" to England, Wales, and Cornwall. The excitement of revival services was propagated in successive waves to the colonies and to those regions where life was hard and traditions were being engulfed by industrialization. The opportunity for emotional participation had a special appeal to the poor, the disadvantaged, the uneducated, and the exploited, those who already felt alienated from conventional modes of worship. The frontier communities of America were surcharged with ideas of self-reliance and freedom. Where mob action was thinly contained by those political institutions still in place, revivalist fervor was welcomed. Here developed those fundamentalist and dionysian enthusiasms central to many otherwise diverse denominations. Much of old church authority went by the board. Liturgy and theology were swept away along with outdated class structures. Those elements that were seen as intellectual, cognitive, humanistic, or classical were explicitly rejected. "Primitive worship" came to be valued and the sermon was replaced by singing, dancing, ecstasy states, possession by the Spirit, speaking in tongues, inspired prophecy, excited interpretation of scripture, healing, and fervid defiance of the Devil and his demons. Spontaneous individual outbursts were encouraged. The acting-out of emotion reflected the anti-authoritarianism and anti-intellectualism of a transitional society.

The deeply felt need for a religion "without the book" or "against the book" found its most urgent expression in the pentecostal churches. A nonintellectual, ecstatic worship was valued not only as reformation, but for bringing individuals closer to the fundamental messages of the Bible, for bringing them into direct contact with God. Speaking unintelligibly "in tongues" was thought a special dispensation of the Almighty, a manifestation coming from him and not from priest or church or intermediary. It was taken as proof of the literal descent of the Holy Spirit into the worshiper, conferring powers of faith and healing.[8]

Holiness-pentecostal congregations emphasized the direct experience of God, the literal possession of the individual by the Spirit, and the ability, conferred by God, to heal, prophesy, and interpret the incomprehensible messages of tongues. These were congruent with the constructs of Sioux religion. The shamans had based their practice on similar beliefs of ancient tradition. The historical Oglalas used a complexly integrated ceremonial system based upon direct entreaty of the supernatural. Individuals sought spiritual power to achieve mastery of an uncertain world. Through the vision quest they sought an identity and direction and symbolic helpers. The *yuwipi* ceremonies involved the summoning of specific spirits. Contact with the supernatural was sought by music and song, including unintelligible "spirit songs." The spirits called upon give the shaman his healing ability directly. Both the shaman and the pentecostal assert the omniscience and omnipotence of spiritual power for all things, including healing. The idea of sovereign efficacy resounds in *yuwipi*, as in charismatic congregations on all continents. The Sioux had no difficulty with the pentecostal view of a personalized Satan and of immediate and literal demons of possession and destruction. Oglala mythology already had names for such personages.

The evangelical pattern of camp meetings and revivals echoes the traditions of the Sioux, much of whose religion was expressed during the gathering of families and bands. The preacher who is ecstatically transported as he describes the fire and blood, the dangers of the devil, baptism by water and tongues of fire, the need to believe and change, continues in the enthusiastic pentecostal religions. Ethical rigor and the avoidance of worldliness are deeply ingrained in the pentecostal creeds as well as in the Sioux tradition, nowhere more clearly than in the puritanism of the newly revitalized Indian Religion and the asceticism advocated by Sioux religious leaders and healers.

Proselytizing Christian churches have found it expedient to incorporate Oglala rites or forms into their liturgy. Stephen E. Feraca described a pentecostal sect at Pine Ridge with a syncretist rite called the "vision quest."[9] The members of the congregation were exhorted to fast for one night with an open Bible. At dawn, if the quest was successful, a passage in Scripture was found underlined by the Holy Spirit. More recently, a fundamentalist church at Wounded Knee was "architecturally adapted from the tipi and the sweat lodge." The pews are arranged in the round with the altar in the center. Timbers in the outer shell imitate lodge poles.

Apart from the healing sects of the fundamentalist denominations, Sioux contacts with Christian churches have had a profound effect on the outward expressions of aboriginal religion. Christian attitudes and practices have been incorporated into the revitalized Sioux Religion. *Wak'aŋ T'áŋka* is equated almost completely with the Christian God and throughout the traditional rites of the Oglalas, as now conducted, are allusions to Christian love and redemption. According to Jake Herman: "The idea of sage being sacred comes from a story from up north. The people saw a man, years ago, who couldn't speak their language. He was a white man, and he had a crown of sage around his head. I don't know—maybe it's just a story." The colored calendar prints of saints wearing halos are common on cabin walls.

Another syncretistic story from a family at Red Shirt Creek contains the biblical idea of bringing forth water from stone:

> There is a story about Stone Valley. One time all the ceremony business was trying to be head of each other. The Mandans, I heard, were the most powerful. The Yankton, Sisseton, Brulé think they are the most powerful. Two medicine men met. It is hard to understand. A little hypnotism figures in here. But anyhow they met. They got talking over how much power they had, how many fasts they had gone through, and what they done. They got through smoking and got to arguing who was the most powerful. The Mandan said, "If you can beat me I'll give you so many head of horses." He took his knife and picked up a stone. Pretty soon water came out. The Brulé took his knife and made a hole above it and blood came out. It's still there— another stone nearby. He said, "If the Great Spirit is with you or me we'll know." He put his hand on the stone and said, "Great Spirit, I love you and I'm helping my people to this day," and took his hand away and it came away with a mark [imprint of the hand in the stone]. The Mandan did it, but it did not go in as deep. So it looks like a man had put two left hands up there. So that shows who was the most powerful. It is in Stone Valley in the east part of the state and it is still there. The Mandan are all gone. I hear there is one or two old ones left. But there are plenty Sioux!

6. Herbalism

Few households in the United States, at least up to the present generation, lacked some treasured herbal remedies. Few communities were without a grandmother who could prepare a root or leaf with alleged curative powers. The same is generally true of Oglala families. "Medicine roots" are sold by vendors at the Dakota fairs and in the small grocery stores. Some elderly women are sought for their extensive knowledge of herbs for illnesses ranging from tuberculosis to heart disease, cancer to depression, nymphomania to pregnancy, and insanity. Beyond this kitchen practice of botanical remedies, however, are those healers who make herbal preparations the mainstay of their therapeutic armamentarium.

Robert Holy Dance, Herbalist

Senior among the herbalists was Robert Holy Dance, a full-blood Brulé from the Rosebud Reservation. In his long career as an indigenous practitioner he treated his rural patients for all their injuries and illnesses. He used botanical remedies traditional in the community, supplemented by the power of his particular spirit healers, which he summoned by drum, song, and prayer. He was an empirical thinker. He developed his skills from case to case and gave much weight to experience. In 1968 he was an aged man, active and garrulous, but with a slight wasting of the face which suggested that he was ill himself. He was an alert observer of the world and his interactions in it. He was a repository of the wisdom of the Sioux, a pungent reporter on the social history of his times, a craftsman, and a naturalist. He made from cedar wood, and was a virtuoso performer on, the long duck-headed Sioux love flutes. His catlinite pipes were majestic in weight and length.

Although Holy Dance was an enrolled resident of the Rosebud Reservation, he often summered on a ranch near Porcupine on the Pine Ridge Reservation. There I came to know him because of his habit of drumming at dawn. The faraway sound was difficult to identify or locate in the half-light of morning. The hoofbeats of my horse obliterated it when we moved, and when we paused to strain our ears, horse and I, it was as tenuous, uncertain, unreal as a distant grouse booming. We found him on the fourth morning on a hillside far above Red Shirt Creek, singing intently and welcoming the sun. Our friendship begun there lasted until his death. We spent many a dawn on that hillside and many a hot afternoon in the shade of the timber farther down. He was the best of talkative companions at the ranch-house table or in his canvas lodge on the creek. He was a good storyteller, endless in gossip and critique. He remembered, or at least talked about, the Ghost Dances of his childhood, the changing fashions in religion thereafter, the slow changes in human population in South Dakota and in the animal life of the ranges and hills. He had a vivid sense of the repetitive quality of politics and people, and seemed to view from a sardonic height their irrational motivations.

His first words to me that morning on the hill were: "Get down and sit. If you listen a long time you can hear the foxes bark. There used to be three of them in the bottom toward White River. Now there are only two." His early-morning observation post gave him information on the habits and movements of birds, the location and condition of the horse herds, the direction of the range stock. He knew the plants in detail, with their signatures (details of botanical anatomy alleged to indicate medical function) and their uses as remedies.

He described his vision experiences and their relationship to his healing powers:

My uncle was Hair Bear. I don't know about the Holy Dance, where that name came from. My vision was—I was walking along, going west, and I crossed a little creek and came to a whole outfit of cabins. Someone was hollering on a knoll, a tall man. He moved. I looked around but he was waving at me. I went over there. There were four old men with white hair standing at the four corners. The tall man was in the center. He said, "They all want to talk to you." I said, *"Ohaŋ"* and shook hands with all of them. They were really old and pitiful. He said, "Young man, if you want to live a long life, look at this valley, with pretty flowers and trees. You see what I show you. Everything is here you can imagine. When anybody calls you, you look at all these things and give them help if you want to live a long life." I bowed my head. *"Ohaŋ!"* I looked again. Across the creek there were a lot of good horses, spotted ponies. He said, "Those are the horses of your relatives. They all have come to life again. So they are living a happy life." That's about all he said to me. I shook hands with all of them and they bowed their heads. I took the same trail back. I bumped something and woke up and thought a lot about it. About six months later a sick man came to me. He had kidney troubles. That was my first step in the herb business. Sometimes I do not get the right herb but I keep it up. In late years I'm trying to get away from that [that is, from errors].

The recognition of the significance of his vision experience was slow-growing. He began to believe his intuitions and to regard them as dependably prophetic.

I've met some wonderful things I didn't understand at first. We went to a steam bath, *inikaġa*, one night, poured water, and had the pipe song. I didn't know what they [the other men present] wanted until then. One of them, his wife was in an Omaha hospital. He wanted to know how she was going to come out. So I said, "Sing four songs," and while we was doing it that woman [the wife] was there in the air [as an apparition], singing with a drum. Later something pushed me like a finger poking my shoulder and said, "That woman is gone." So I said to him, "You will see her next day." I did not tell him it would be in a casket. I just couldn't tell him. Sure enough, she came the next day in a casket. I can do those things in a sweat bath. I don't like to tell them things straight out. *Inikaġa* is the sweat bath. It is "you-make-your-life" or "making life." *Ini* is "life."

The *T'uŋkaśila*—the grandfathers—and the *yuwipi* spirits make prophecy possible:

Once at a *yuwipi* a man had his hand out. One of the gourds put a glass stone in his hand. It is a good luck stone. I said, "Put it in a buckskin; when you need good luck on a trip or something you look at it and wish good luck." And he did. And when he loses it his luck is gone. The guy [the *yuwipi* man conducting the ceremony] did not even know the gourds gave him the glass stone.

The identity and number of spirit helpers is variable, to some extent unpredictably, to some extent depending on the power of the shaman:

There is only about five spirits comes in to each ceremony. Every *yuwipi* [man] knows who is coming in. They are all different for each *yuwipi*. Yellow Horse was always with me [as a spirit]. It's a long time [that is, an old story], a man who was to be with me all the time. He died about one hundred and fifty years ago. Poor Thunder told me, and how did he know I was telling the story about Yellow Horse? He was a good medicine man. He was honest and kept out of crooked business. He just wanted to help people.

Almost every conversation about spirit power was interrupted again and again by warnings about its correct use:

Things to be avoided include like some guy wanted to spark a girl, or jealousy [a complaint of jealousy], or finding things. A regular medicine man tries to keep away from

Herbalism 127

that stuff because he will lose power. Those guys who do this other work do not live very long. Like you want good luck with gambling or something, or making something so you will have good luck. *Wap'iya,* that is. A healer is different from a charm maker. There is pipe songs and *yuwipi* songs, and *heyok'a* songs when someone wants to find out about the weather. The *heyok'a* comes in and tell you things you never heard of. They can even tell where there is going to be a car wreck, or something happen like that.

Maturity and wisdom:

Crow Dog [a contemporaneous Brulé medicine man] is pretty good. They don't go into that stuff until they are solid in their thinking. About thirty-five. Healers aren't young guys.

Misuse of a prescription:

All kinds of womens been coming to me for their kidneys. I'm very careful about giving medicine to a woman. She's got to be toward her forties before I give her kidney medicine. Got to be sure they not pregnant. I give that medicine and it's a workout [cathartic]. It cleans out thoroughly, and they're okay. Must be they are with different kind of men all the time. They ask me to come here for medicine. They say, "Very good! Very good medicine!" So that kind of a deal [inadvertently causing abortion] I don't know anything about until later. A few had gallstones in their kidneys. I can pulverize them so they pass out without an operation.

Holy Dance returned again and again, always with disapproval, to the problems caused by promiscuity:

I'm not surprised they have disease. All kinds of disease. From womens. It's intersex. It's because women are crazy for sex. Terrible! They go with so many men. Sex crazy so their womb is all filthy and goes to the kidneys. It is an herb I give them. There is three or four kinds of mint. One is for swelling in the belly or wherever it is. *C'eyaka,* that's peppermint.

Many of his preparations were given with little discrimination. A strong cathartic served for kidney trouble, both infections and stones. Other preparations were somewhat more specific:

> Doctors have a big problem with anemia. When your blood turns to water. We got a medicine, a root, for that. One cupful would cure you, bring back all your corpuscles. There is a morning root and an evening root. *Wep'ac'ap'a,* that's anemia. It has to be used just so.
>
> There is a plant that is near water. It has purple with a yellow center, and two leaves. It has milk. It is for poison ivy. Jealous weed has a small bur, fuzzy. It's for sore throat. You make a poultice, like flax. It will bust quinsy from closing up your throat. It is small, very little, and fuzzy. Big as a bean. Each with a little hook that holds on. Sunflowers are for diarrhea. Boil the leaves. There is several things for that diarrhea business. Or stomach out of order. I have a medicine for that.

Some of his experiences frightened him and others, and set limits upon his use of the *wak'aŋ*:

> I been going to these here *yuwipi* forty years. I know who is right and who isn't. They sing the pipe song and the medicine song and whatever songs they come there for. Once I was in a sweat lodge [with] no women anywhere. But I heard a woman there singing with a friend, and I knew his wife had died. I had so much power [in that sweat lodge] I scared everybody in there. I didn't want to scare anyone. So I gave it [*yuwipi*] up. I just do the medicine part and the sweat lodge part, and to help in the Sun Dance, to help guide them.

Holy Dance did not expect to have a successor: "No, nobody gonna follow me. My grandson isn't old enough to catch onto all this stuff, although he has been at the sweat lodge. He got scared of the wind, the ghosts, while he was keeping the door."

Herbalism 129

Like other ritualists, he repeatedly emphasized that meticulous attention must be paid to the details of a vision and that ritual powers are strictly delimited. "If you try to go beyond it, it does not work. One medicine man was getting good, but by exceeding his power he had a fatal car wreck." Another healer was ineffective because he tried to do too much—"peyote and *yuwipi* and everything. That weakens it."

The *p'ejuta* doctor dispenses substances, usually herbal, in addition to the magical or spiritual ministrations emphasized in the activities of other types of healers. Holy Dance said:

I give medicines and I got two stones, for muscle and bones troubles. Or for a stroke. I've cured four people on strokes. Mouth and neck twisted, just like that, I got them out of it in ten minutes. I used my stones on it. I found my stones. They glow in the night, from radium or something like that. I put them in hot water and put my hand in hot water and put it where you have the trouble. . . . There is all kinds of strokes. Suppose you went down there in the dark and someone gave you a bad punch. That's a stroke. Or if you got too hot and drank something cold, that's a stroke, too. In winter and your teeth chatter and you get up quick, you get a different kind of stroke. You feel your tongue is going to come out.

The stones were also good for colds: "For this you grind up the stone and boil it a little. It works."

Animals in nature and in their supernatural manifestations figured large in Holy Dance's thinking. As a field naturalist he was a fountain of observation, and his ritual life used animal imagery:

Indians really go by owls. Once twenty-five or thirty owls met in the evening. One was old and spotted. So old he couldn't make a noise. They went two over there, two over there. Finally only he was left. Pretty soon you hear them hooting, way over there, over there. If they hear a spotted owl something is going to happen, and it's true. I was a forest ranger in those times. I never got scared. A spotted owl will talk, just like a person. So Indians go by owls, and I use it for that medicine business.

Iktomi, the Trickster of Sioux mythology, had attributes of deceptiveness and hostility toward humans which made him especially dangerous:

Indians is very superstitious about hypnotizing. Hypnotizing is very dangerous. *Waħte! Watch out! Iktomi p'ejuta,* that's spider medicine. The mink was *yuwipi* medicine.

This woman, she had this power. They accused her of various things. I took up for her. She wanted to give me all her outfit. "Pretty soon I am going to go in the ground," she said. She wanted to give it all to me. Said she did not use it for six or eight years, but wouldn't tell me why. "Others can tell you," she said. It turned out her kids all died, one by one [because of the power]. So I was lucky I didn't take it.

Another woman took one part of it and turned it into a ghost medicine. She had the power, you know, through her doings, this second lady. You go through, and when everything's through, everything is in order, all tied up and rolled up. The last thing is the pipe, and nobody can find it, and the person she is doctoring is sitting on it and don't know it. So I don't know. But she did not live very long, so I know she was using the pipe the wrong way. The first woman got it from a vision, like I got mine, and you have to go by it.

That's *Iktomi.* Dangerous because you don't know what he will do.

An acute observer of the natural world, he still believed popular "snake stories," derived from ancient mythology:

You been at all those museums in Washington? Did you ever see a woman give birth to five snakes? They are all alive. They got them in the museum in Washington. A long time ago. A lot of these stories, I don't know. More holy than anything else, maybe. I've known of women keeping snakes for pets. An old woman had one. She had a place like a sweat lodge. A kid shot him [the snake] when she was gone, in the mouth. Kids then was always shooting arrows. When she came back she said, "Who killed your grandfather?" She got a young man to bury him. And it was his real grandfather.

Assessing the future and acting on one's intuitions:

Indians used to be good at fortunetelling. Something that's going to happen. A man got his medicine out, rubbed it or smoked over it before he went to bed, about something that was going to happen the next day. They don't do that anymore.

Local whites were quick to give testimonials to the efficacy of Holy Dance's remedies. Orville Schwarting, a rancher, told me:

Holy Dance's wife died in May 1969. There is a year of mourning, then a feast and giveaway, an honoring ceremony, and then she is free. The soul stays around three days, following the person most loved. Or if something is wrong it is around a long time. The giveaway terminates the life. Bob's [Holy Dance's] wife saved everything—Christmas presents, birthday presents, all that stuff—for years, to provide a good giveaway. Everybody was given valuable things. My wife went. There were many dedications and gifts of money. After that, he had a stroke two years ago. He resisted the specialists who wanted to operate on his eyes, and got over it himself. Also, he decided one day he didn't want his wheelchair and he left it. He is a remarkable man. I went to Wanblee with him and I joked he couldn't stop the kind of storm that was coming, but he moved his hand and the storm stayed on one side the whole way. He is amazing!

A white ranch wife's testimonial:

Holy Dance has a baked leaf preparation for sinusitis. It is burned and inhaled. He has absolute cures even in people who go to doctors when they live in town. He treats everybody. We don't need a doctor when he is around. He treats anybody and they always get better.

Other Herbalists

Holy Dance told about a medicine woman he had known:

> There was a medicine woman, *wap'iya wíŋyaŋ*. She had beads. She would look up and each one would turn into a bird and fly around. Then turn into beads again. She was a relative. She tried to give me her whole outfit. She said, "You are a good man and should have this." I told her I would give her fifty cents to show me. She had three deals. The *yuwipi* and maybe she hypnotized me. I keep thinking about that. She had three stuffed mink. When she was going to doctor, she'd hit them on the ground and they'd come alive. They was stuffed but they'd hop like they was alive. She was a real medicine woman.

A representative of the Tribal Council supervising the Sun Dance said:

> A woman named Tobacco, of the Pretty Hip family, is an herb woman. She collects all the old-time plants. She can give you a cure for anything if you get to know her. She lives in a cabin up beyond White Clay Creek where it goes into the river. She knows everything that is good for you.

Some Herbal Remedies

Many of the medicinals used by the Oglalas are of uncertain identity. The botanical preparations, or "cures," have local names, but it is infrequent that the roots, broken leaves and stems, and crumbled flowerheads can be connected with the living plant or the place where it was collected. The herbalists have their own collections, gathered with prayers. There are a significantly large number of preparations for dysentery and diarrhea, reflecting the prevalence of those maladies. The following list gives some of the ways in which plant materials are handled.

Some are said to be specifics, some are sovereign, all are empirical. I have identified scientific names where possible. Lakota terms are from Father Eugene Buechel's Lakota dictionary (1970). The quotations are from a number of individuals, especially Stephen Gay and Holy Dance. Frances Afraid of Hawk lent me her book of plant notes and specimens.

Lak'olwak'alyapi ["Sioux boiled drink"] (*Coreopsis*?). "The flowers and stems are boiled and strained, and used for diarrhea, gallbladder, and kidney trouble."

mak'uyazaŋpi ["chest illness"] (*Juncaceae*). "It is boiled and given as a fast cure for diarrhea."

uŋkcela ["cactus"] (*Lophophora williamsii,* peyote). "It is used in the form of a prayer. This medicine is said to cure almost everything. It is used to take away pain and make a quick recovery."

c'aŋli icahiye ["tobacco mixer"]. "A root from Montana. It is used to flavor tobacco and is used for the throat and chest, for bronchitis, and is boiled and rubbed on the face to relieve sores. The smell goes all through the house and will repel snakes."[1] Pieces of this woody root are for sale at country general stores.

azilyapi ["incense"]. Sweetgrass or any incense. "Comes from Minnesota" and is sold by itinerant peddlers.

c'eyaka ("mint"). "There are four kinds. One, peppermint, is used for swellings."

c'aŋsiŋsila ["fat wood"]. "A root which is used to cure headaches." (Buechel suggests this might be camomile.)[2]

suŋkleja ["dog (horse) urination"]. A tea brewed from the dried leaves is given to individuals who cannot urinate. "It cures the infection, and in a few minutes the person urinates." (Buechel identifies this as a milk vetch.)[3]

hoksic'ekpa ["baby navel, twin"] (puffball fungus). This powder is used to dry up the navel of newborn infants and to dry up fever blisters. It stops bleeding and nosebleeding. (Buechel also identifies this as the pasqueflower, as well as other species.)[4]

wagmu p'ejuta ["squash medicine"]. The seeds are pounded up and boiled for use as kidney medicine or as a general cure-all.

p'ejihota ["gray grass"] (*artemisia,* silver sage). "It is made into a tea used for tuberculosis, for pain in the ears, head, chest, and stomach, and for diarrhea and colds. It is used in form of prayer."

icahpehu ["whip stem"] (*Echinacea angustifolia*). "The dried leaf is mashed or chewed and put on a toothache." Country children try to trick visiting children into chewing the root. It imparts an unpleasant numbing of the mouth tissues, which is the basis of its use for toothache. (Buechel identifies it as the purple coneflower.)[5]

pteiciyuha (*Compositaceae*). "The flower heads is a tea for colds and kidney trouble and pain."

sinkpe t'awote ["muskrat's food"] (calamus). It is "used for colds, sore throat, toothache." Holy Dance noted that it is also used "to make dogs mean [i.e., better watchdogs, although others report a calming effect at lower dosages]. But too much makes them crazy. It comes from the Sisseton Reservation, or from Minnesota. You go in water up to your hips, where the cattails grow. You can smell it. The smell leads you to it. It is good for infection in the tonsils and it helps singers. You can talk and sing better if you chew on a piece of it, like if you are going to make a long speech. Suck it or powder it and drink it."

poip'iye ["to heal swelling"]. Boiled into tea, it is put on sores, swellings, and snakebite. "It gives off a cooling sensation."

wahpeak'ikaskapi ["flowers tied together"] (*Clematis*). The white flowers of the vine are boiled "for swellings and to ease the tonsils." (Buechel identifies it as common hops.)[6]

In 1901 George Sword's ten-medicine collection included *sinkpe t'awote* and *icahpehu*; James R. Walker, who recorded his information, identified the latter as "the pith of soapweed" (yucca).[7]

Cʻaŋli Icahiye

My attempts to identify *cʻaŋli icahiye* exemplify the problems of ethnobotanical study of Sioux medicines. Ella Irving, an Oglala, investigated its use and kindly sent me her notes. She reported: "This is the most popular Sioux medicine. It is chewed for toothache and sore throats, made into cough syrup, chewed and spit on the hot stones in the sweat lodge to provide a decongestant vapor, used in the treatment of earaches, burned as a purifying incense, and singers like to chew it to keep their voices strong."

Cʻaŋli icahiye is widely known and used. When purchased from medicine vendors it is kept in decorated containers and handled ritually. Its botanical identity could not be determined from the dried parts, and its specific provenance seems to be unknown except to those who gather it. It is not collected locally. Two pharmacological laboratories were unable to identify it, and a botanical review served only to increase the list of possibilities. Many members of the *Umbelliferae,* for example, have aromatic, edible, or toxic roots. George Bird Grinnell lists *Leptotaenia multifida* as a "tonic" medicinal of the Cheyennes, western neighbors of the Sioux. Grinnell also gives *Osmorhiza longistylis Torr.* and *O. obtusa* (Coutl. and Rose)—both known as sweet cicely—as having aromatic roots used for stomach and urinary disorders. Per Axel Rydberg's *Flora of the Prairies and Plains* lists *O. longistylis* as having a root with an anise aroma, and *Cogswellia* (*Lomatium*) as the edible biscuit root. Walter B. McDougall and Herman A. Baggley's *The Plants of Yellowstone National Park* gives "indian balsam," *Leptotaenia dissecta* var. *multifida* (*Lomatium dissectum*) with large edible roots, and "sweet root" as *Osmorhiza*. It says *Heracleum* is used "ceremonially as well as for food." Robert H. Lowie writes that the Crows used *Leptotaenia multifida Nutt.* as an incense at ceremonies and as a cureall, and alludes to ritual use and smoking of "bear root" and "wild carrot incense."[8]

Herbal Treatment of a Sexual Disorder

The Brulé medicine man William Schweigman, a Sun Dancer at Pine Ridge, practiced herbal therapies. He described the value of a decoction of *Symphorocarpus* (buckbrush), a common plant that grows in thickets and bears clusters of white berries. He used the leaves and berries to treat nymphomania. When I incautiously questioned him about the wisdom of interfering in that interesting condition, he dismissed my frivolity and emphasized its exceeding seriousness in his experience.

Herbal Treatment of Congestive Heart Disease

A fifty-two-year-old Oglala, employed by the Tribal Council, entered a hospital in a nearby city after several severe attacks ascribed to heart disease. He left against medical advice a week later to haul lumber and supplies for the Sun Dance. He continued to have severe chest pain and feelings of collapse. He went back to the hospital and was told that readmission was urgent. Instead, he had a *p'ejuta* woman make an herb tea, which he kept in a fruit jar on the seat of his truck. Whenever he felt faint, a few sips of the tea seemed to help. He continued to work hard during the hot summer days and celebrated vigorously as usual at the Sun Dance. He drank heavily with friends. While stringing electrical wires on the roof of a building he became so dizzy and blinded that he almost fell off. Otherwise, he said, "The Indian medicine makes me feel good, except my ankles stay swole. There ain't no use going to town to a hospital. I don't want to stay there."

The material given here on Oglala herbalism is anecdotal. Fortunately, several systematic studies are available. Father Eugene Buechel's Lakota dictionary includes extensive commentaries on ethnobotany, giving Lakota names and traditional uses of many prairie plants. Buechel's plant collections, which still exist, have been reviewed by Dilwyn J. Rogers. Stephen E. Feraca gives in detail the ceremony and prayers used in collecting *p'ejutap'a,* "bitter medicine" (*Parosela aurea*) and the use of *icaħpehu* as a tea and as an infusion sprayed on the patient's chest from the mouth of the healer. He emphasized that to the Oglala herbalist every plant has its putative remedial function, and that only persons of designated powers may gather and use them with impunity.[9]

Oglala Herbalism

The Oglala herbalist is nearer in his rationale of therapy to systems familiar to white experience than are other Oglala healers. European herbalism antedates classical and medieval medicine. Empirical botanical therapists like the sixteenth-century physician Parcelsus were in the mainstream of accepted practice. Because the Lakota herbalist generally utilizes a simplistic empiricism—"this is good for that"—and tends to be untroubled by a coherent theory of etiology or a plausible body of experience, his reliance on magical manipulation is often visible to the skeptical eye. His realm of therapeutic endeavor may be difficult to separate from quackery. The Appalachian "yarb doctor," the Chinese herbalists in American cities, the herb women in rural communities, and almost anybody's grandmother provide most of us with an experience with an herbal therapist. My druggist in Washington, D.C., for example, although trained in science, sold ginseng root too, and had an enthusiastic sales pitch about its efficacy. His shelves creaked with other patent medicines that he had no qualms about selling. Physicians who collaborate with him in magic, and with an uncritical acceptance of label information, dispense preparations that have nothing to do with science. They are the surviving herbalists of our prescientific past.

The Sioux *p'ejuta* doctor exemplified by Holy Dance is something more than an herbalist. Holy Dance made frequent allusions to hypnosis and pondered whether the subject or the hypnotist was deluded. His references to autosuggestion, human-to-animal transformations, and ghostly influence invited patients to think about the nature of their disorders in addition to swallowing the medicament. It is hard to know whether Holy

Dance exceeded the Western physician in his fundamental respect for the magic of pill and powder. The overflowing medicine cabinets of American homes and the drug clutter of the streets suggest we have a public willing to abandon rationality in favor of mysticism. As a provider of materia medica the Oglala herbalist seems to be carrying on a tradition common to many cultures, but he cannot be separated from the rest of the Sioux medical-religious structure. The *p'ejuta* man may also practice *yuwipi* and use the sweat lodge, pipe songs, and other rites. Although herbal practitioners make extensive and explicit use of medicinal preparations, other healers may rely exclusively on ritual.

7. *Heyokᶜa*

Heyokᶜa dreamers and the Sioux "contrary cult" stand in ambiguous relationship to the healing arts. On one hand, their activities are directed at the protection of the community and the *heyokᶜa* dances are performed "for the health and safety of all the people." On the other hand, individual *heyokᶜa* are said to have the power to reverse the healing effects of any ritual, regimen, or remedy, and medical treatment ought properly to be deferred when they are present.

The *heyokᶜa* is an ancient, loosely organized, at least partly secret society. The members assert specific magical powers pertaining to war, the hunt, and healing. The *heyokᶜa*, or contraries, are an integral part of the religious and ceremonial system, and *heyokᶜa* individuals have a well-defined role in Oglala daily life as well. By systematically breaking the customs and prohibitions of the community the contrary achieves a personal mysteriousness that translates into the magical and the sacred. In Sioux society a puritanical moral code and pressure for conformity to social values are channeled into character development by ridicule and shaming. When, for example, the tensions of this process become intolerable, the *heyokᶜa* is an incarnation of relief. His presence is a counterbalance to conformity. He is simultaneously useful and dangerous, his origins are mysterious, and his functions are enigmatic.

Becoming *heyokᶜa* is involuntary and unavoidable. Traditionally, dream or vision quest images interpreted as symbolic of the

Thunder Beings (lightning, water, the god *Heyok'a* or his representatives) obligated the dreamer to specific lifestyles and activities. He was expected to observe extreme generosity to the point of self-poverty. By elaborate contrary and backwards behaviors he countered the dangers of lightning and storm. These terrors of the firmament embody the wrath of the *wak'aŋ síca,* the destructive powers of the Oglala spirit world. The *heyok'a* did everything in reverse fashion to neutralize them, in an elaborate reverse magic against disaster. On ceremonial days the masked *heyok'a* dancers brought apprehension and laughter into solemn proceedings. Like the archetypal clown, they fomented anxiety, denial, distortion, and avoidance in their onlookers. They personified disorder, deviancy, contrariness, and unpredictability. In recent years *heyok'a* costumes have burlesqued Caucasians and blacks, or intoxicated Indians. Some *heyok'a* carried ludicrous equipment and decorations, wore pendulous penislike noses, and affected disgusting or insane behaviors. Although their negative magic against death by storm and lightning bolt was professedly practiced for the good of the entire band, the more conservative Oglalas seemed to feel that the *heyok'a*'s disruptive influence outweighed their potential benefit.

The social functions of the designated fool have drawn the attention of many writers. He has a long history in classical and European cultures. He is found in South America and Africa, always related to medicine and ceremony. In North America he appears in many forms and variants. The sacred clowns of the Chiricahua Apaches and Mescalero Apaches, to focus on only one example, were curing shamans. Their dangerous aspects dictated that they be consulted only in dire circumstances. These Apache personages wore long-beaked masks and practiced disruptive, objectionable, opposite, and antinatural behaviors. Their destructive role required them to learn and to observe meticulously a vast body of orthodox ritual procedure. They were the arbiters and enforcers of rules, customs, and liturgical sequences, reminding us once again that the oppositional character has to be well versed in the dogma he opposes. Another example, the Pueblo and Mayo-Yaqui sacred clowns whose pub-

lic behaviors included feces eating and simulated coition, had a multitude of functions, including healing. Elsie Clews Parsons and Ralph L. Beals drew parallels between the contrary clowns and *heyok'a* of the western American tribes and the ritualized foolhardiness in battle of some of the war societies of those tribes. The accounts of Wilson D. Wallis and James Owen Dorsey emphasize the healing accomplishments of the Sioux *heyok'a* without saying how the healing was done. Wallis gives a number of stories about the contrariness of the *heyok'a* but observes that they were simultaneously the most powerful of medicine people.[1] Lakota *heyok'a* of today are not disturbed by an unexplained gap between their badness and goodness, burlesques and beneficence.

Historical Aspects of the Heyok'a

The papers of James R. Walker include a description and drawings of *heyok'a* warriors. Walker recorded that the *heyok'a* were able to inflict skin disease and sore eyes, and he gives extended descriptions of the nature of the *Wakiŋyaŋ* dreamers, their attributes, function, and rituals. During the times of tribal combat the horned buffalo warbonnet was the identifying mark of the *heyok'a*. Lightning streaks painted on rider and mount represented the vision experience of the Thunderers. Among the Crows, in contrast, the insignia of the equivalent ritualist was a decrepit bow and arrow or a useless gun, as if the *akbiarusacanica* had become the antithesis of the warrior. Black Elk, who was himself a *heyok'a*, a Thunder dreamer, and a *yuwipi*, described the Lakota *heyok'a* ceremony. His account suggests that the *heyok'a* provided to the community a psychologically constructive influence, holding up a smiling, humorous image when the people were in despair and a weeping, cynical, or admonitory face "when they are feeling too good and are too sure of feeling safe."[2] There was a hortatory function in the clown's destruction of order and its subsequent restitution in the context of ceremony. He brought a balance to solemnity, and by violation of all taboos he aped the sins of adults and the misbehaviors of children. He was an institutionalized imp and madman, a stylized deviant who made all transgressions manifest, then left the stage to his betters.

The early historical Oglala *heyok'a* seems to have been a warrior with extraordinary magical powers. He exhibited exceptional feats of bravery, rode against the enemy, and killed in the service of the security of the tribe. His violent behavior as a warrior was strictly proscribed within the band but brought honor, status, and power when externalized. With the end of tribal warfare the *heyok'a* became, at some unknown point, a masked ritualist, magically brave still, immune to fire and boiling water, whose chant and ceremony were in the service still of tribal well-being.

But why the mask and anonymity? The contrary's negativistic and revolting behavior carried a heavy social price for the individual despite his useful functions of underlining those actions expressly prohibited to normal people. The mask allowed some degree of distancing from an onerous role. With or without mask, the *heyok'a*'s backwards speech and action constantly emphasized, by reversal, the prevailing standards of social behavior. The ambivalence of his magic was always clear: he was dangerous at close focus and beneficent in overview. He could preserve the *t'iyoṡpaye,* or extended family, the basic unit of Lakota social organization, and wreak havoc upon the medical treatment of the individual. He could risk injury to himself and others by making pretend war charges into unarmed crowds. He enticed bystanders to throw water at him so that he could retaliate by drawing down thunder, lightning, storm, and death upon them. He may yet be shown, if it is not already too late for the inquiry, to be fundamentally related to the giveaway ceremony, which may be, at one level, a reverse magic against plunder. No scholar has yet examined this possible dynamic, leaving the ritual to be explained as an assertion of social status and a redistribution of goods.

If it is true that the *heyok'a* were warriors, warriors most adept at feats of bravery, when was masking and anonymity introduced? I know of no evidence to answer, but Robert Holy Dance contended: "The old *heyok'a*s at Ghost Dance times had a round mask with a large beak. They had three eagle feathers on the head and two side streamers that came together on the back." Almost all of his thought about *heyok'a* centered on their magical powers:

The Indians used to have *Iktomi* stories. Once these old fellows were telling about a *heyok'a*. The people had a stone about so high. They were arguing about what kind of stone it was. It wasn't very thick, but an odd shape. Not pipestone, but like it. There was a little hill, a little away, a few trees on it. A *heyok'a* peeked over the hill. He told the people he was going to shoot. He said to clear away. The arrow had not stone or bone but a rawhide tip. This *heyok'a* peeked up about four times, no noise, with a quick motion. He shot the arrow through the stone. The *heyok'a* disappeared. The arrow stayed in the stone all night. The next day they got a medicine man to find out what it means. He made a performance and said, "Another *heyok'a* will come to take the arrow out." They couldn't pull it out at all.

The next day another *heyok'a* peeked four times and made a motion to them to pull the arrow out. One man said, "It must be me because I got the medicine man." It came right out. The *heyok'a* made a motion like that, for the man to throw the arrow towards him. He picked it up and went over the hill.

That was when I was twenty-five years old and they was talking about those way-long-time deals when they was young. One of the men was a medicine man. He said it must mean something, and had the ceremony to find out the meaning. I never got what it meant.

But the *heyok'a* is dying off, the guys who belong to that organization. One died last year. He used to do it [perform as a *heyok'a*] every year. He did a lot of things. He could take a whip and crack it under his leg and make the sparks fly, dancing at night. That's a real thing, there. That's real something!

Later, Holy Dance wrote to me concerning the *heyok'a*:

I will do my best to explain the Heyuka ceremony. The purpose of the ceremony is to pray for health among people, [alleviation of] starvation among animals or maybe [relief from] dry weather which would cause a drouth.

A person who has a dream or vision will perform the ceremony. The Heyuka ceremony is much different from the Yuepe, Horse Dance, sundance, and Eagle ceremony. It is the most sorrowful of ceremonies. I will state here that I have seen the Heyuka ceremony performed fifty-four years ago. It was the last one performed by the Sioux. These five ceremonies were performed as far back as two hundred years, according to my great uncle who lived to be one hundred years old.

I have drawn a pictograph of the Heyuka ceremony so you can understand it better.

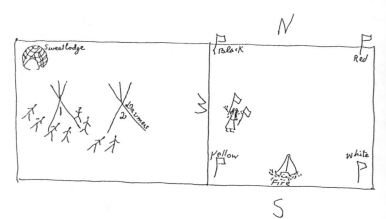

The ceremony is performed in daylight in a space fifty yards wide and one hundred yards long. This will be in two sections. In the west section you will see a sweat house and near the center there are two tipis. Eight or more persons take part in the ceremony besides the person performing it.

He or she takes a sweat bath the evening before the day of the ceremony. The other eight persons take a sweat bath just before the ceremony. When the eight people are through with their baths, they go to tipi number one, where they dress in different styles and wear masks. This group is now the Heyuka. Two of the Heyukas go to tipi number two where they will stay and sing throughout the ceremony.

In the east section there are four flags in each corner. [At] The north corner [is] a black flag, east corner a red, south corner a white, and west corner a yellow flag. These four flags represent the four winds and also the health of the people, the weather, medicine, and preventing the animals from vanishing away. In the west part of the east section there are two flags, blue and green, blue for heaven and green for the earth.

There will be two heyukas running from the tipi number one toward the first place [fireplace]. At the south side of the east section there is a fireplace where they will cook a dog. The person that will perform the ceremony according to the vision will dress in white, with her hair hanging, and will be barefoot.

Now she stands before the two flags which represent heaven and earth, with her arm raised she prays to the great spirit. In the meantime the two Heyukas at the fireplace will build a fire, so they cook a dog. The dog is dressed and cleaned at the sweat house, the remains is burned up at the sweat bath fire.

Now the six heyukas are behind her helping her pray. The singers in tipi number two start singing several different songs. [During] The first song, she goes to the north flag which is black and prays. Then she comes back to the two center flags. As another song comes up she goes to the east flag which is red and stands there praying till they sing another song. Then she goes back to the center flags and they sing another song; she goes to the south white flag and goes back to the center flags. As they sing another song she goes to the yellow flag. They sing still another song and she goes to the fireplace. She goes around the fire four times as the six Heyukas follow her. They go back to the center flags. She then goes back to the fireplace and stands there praying. Meanwhile the six heyukas are dancing around the fireplace four times, they dance according to the songs. They go back to the center flags. Four of the heyukas dance back to the west where the tipis are. The other two heyukas dance toward the fireplace to fix the fire and see about the cooking dog. Then the two dance back to the tipis. A different song is sung and she faces the west to watch the six heyukas dance.

They dance for about twenty minutes. Then another song comes up. With the six heyukas behind her she makes motions toward the four winds and heaven and earth. Making the same motions the heyukas will start dancing toward the fireplace. The heyukas will dance four times around the fire making motions according to the song. After this they then dance toward the two flags and line up behind her. The singers sing a sad song as she starts marching toward the fireplace. There are three heyukas on each side of her. She is crying as she marches. The heyukas will run around looking for some grass or weeds, then running back to her they will rub her hands with it.

Almost to the fireplace, the heyukas stop dancing, but she marches on to the pot with the cooking dog in it. When she gets to the pot, she makes motions to the four winds, heaven and earth. The heyukas are also making the motions.

With her bare hands she reaches in the pot of boiling soup, and pulls off [out] the dog's head! She points it to the four winds, heaven and earth and walks toward the crowd of people.

If anyone in the crowd belong[s] to that organization, they will rush toward her taking the dog head, which is very hot.

She then marches back to the two flags with the heyuka where they will pray. The singers then stop singing and go back to the tipi number one. The heyuka will lead the woman to tipi number two where they will leave her. They then go back to tipi number one and the ceremony is over.

In this heyuka ceremony, pipe and tobacco knots are not used. I might add here that the woman's hands are not scalded or burned.

The Boiling-Water Feat

Melvin R. Gilmore says: "The leaves of the prairie mallow, when chewed, yield a mucilaginous fluid which, when rubbed on the hands, forms a coating enabling one to plunge the hands quickly into hot water without being scalded. This is used by the Arikaras to protect their hands in similar ceremonies."[3] Prairie mallow, or "yellow rose," is *Dasiphora fruticosa* Rydb. The Oglalas say another plant, the globe mallow or scarlet mallow, is their source of protection in the boiling water feat. The Lakota name is *útahu c'aŋhloǵaŋ,* the botanical is *Malvastrum coccinea Pursh. (Sphaeralcea coccinea* (Nut.) Rydb.).

This plausible account has taken on the authority of truth, often repeated and divorced from reality. A hog butcher from Asturias recently described to me his method for ascertaining the heat of water for scalding carcasses: "If you can plunge your arm in three times without burning, it's not quite hot enough. Anybody can do the same." So much for mallow and magic and for being in on the secret.

Healing and Heyok'a

Holy Dance's detailed description of ceremonial procedure says less than we would like to know about the healing function of the *heyok'a.* Joe and Ben White Face, Oglalas at Porcupine, emphasized to me that a *wic'aśa wak'aŋ,* a holy or sagacious man, can be a *heyok'a* but a *heyok'a,* although "spiritual," is not a healer-shaman. An apparently opposite view is expressed in J. L. Smith's description of the preparation of offering cloths for the Sacred Calf Pipe, where black as a symbol and as an offering "represented the west and the *Heyokas,* Thunder Clowns. It was hoped they would add their powers [to the prayers]."[4] Smith wrote to me in 1969 about a *yuwipi* ceremony held during a thunderstorm, at the end of which a ninety-year-old man drew him aside and whispered, "It is a good night for *heyok´a*s, so be very careful driving back to your camp."

One official of the Pine Ridge Sun Dance, who had many duties of building and scheduling and served as the public announcer, understandably liked to see things running smoothly from dawn to midnight. The *heyok´a* were an annoyance to him. "*Heyok´a*s are guys who went on a vision quest and by some type of supernatural power he was given some type of power to heal the sick with herb or root. But personally I don't like them at a dance and if I had my way about it I would skin their asses out of there. I just don't like them, and there is getting to be more and more of these fellows!"

The dangerous potential felt to reside in the *heyok´a* is alluded to in a description by Howard of a clown Sun Dance held on the Turtle Mountain Reservation in North Dakota in 1960. This variant ritual was "dreamed" by two of its sponsors. It was considered to be highly powerful and highly dangerous. It was conducted by beak-masked personages, with reversals of all parts of the traditional Sun Dance ceremony.[5]

The Dynamics of the Ritual Clown

If one observes the social fool and the clown in daily life (easy enough, you might say), in literature and clinic, and in his ceremonial manifestations, one's early conclusions are that his variegated qualities are confusing and make him appear ever more enigmatic. This delays an understanding of his psychological and perhaps mythological origins. Let us look for a model that might explain the clown-fool as an abstract phenomenon, applicable to many settings. From this we may find a clarification of his particular expression as a Teton *heyok´a*.

Suppose that the ritual life of any human group is constructed on magical ideas from the past. These are the group's medicine, from which supernatural forces emanate. Consider that the group is supported in its culture, tradition, and custom by rules of social behavior expressed as taboos. A central proscription stands against internecine violence. Its observance is crucial to continued group survival. Expressed as a taboo against blood, it protects against the consequences of internal aggression. In its elaborations it serves to limit consanguinity, incest, and menstrual sexuality, and is operative in rules of kinship and defilement. Orthodox power is based on inheritance, the conservation of elite blood. All of this, so far at least, has numerous parallels in Teton ethnology.

Next consider the enigma of the ritual clown-fool-contrary. In the abstract and cross-culturally, he seem to be a subsidiary or even incidental ritualist, but his behaviors are extraordinarily conspicuous. He systematically violates accepted custom. He is silly, noisy, hyperactive. He is frightening by his very strangeness. One might suppose there is a method in his antics, but for twenty-five hundred years writers have remained in the audience, so to speak, describing the clown without understanding him. Aristotle in the *Poetics* (VII) took note of his masks, phallic songs and processions, coarse invective, flaunted ugliness and deformities, and obscenities intended to ward off evil. The Attic fool followed the Empire into Europe and stayed on as jester, court fool, Abbot of Disorder, and circus clown. Centuries of children have cried at first encounter with these gesticulating zanies and remained fascinated and half-comprehending the rest of their lives. Who is this irrepressible and ubiquitous character? What does he do so endlessly that we seem unable to do without?

Roger Caillois first pointed out the ritual significance of transgression, and Laura Makarius utilized this insight to make explicit the true nature of the ritual clown.[6] He is the specialist in oppositional behavior. His magical (religious) potency derives not only from his ability to ignore without harm the prohibitions to which normal people are inextricably bound, but also from his peculiarly "suspended" status. He is outside society, outside normality, and forever awaits ceremonial redefinition and return. The contrary disobeys every rule, and he obscures the defiance of blood taboos under a whirlstorm of less important reversals. He and no other can make mock attacks with dangerous weapons upon his fellows. He and no other is immune to abhorrence of blood. He manipulates it, symbolically or in actuality, as food, drink, weapon, or medicine. He is as counter-phobic regarding blood as the "crazy" warriors were regarding combat danger.

This model of a reversal ritualist fits the Sioux *heyok'a* passing well. A few details will improve it further. Medicine men are painstakingly careful to explain that menstruating women cannot participate in ceremony; for blood to be present is dangerous and leads invariably to bad outcomes. Medicine men make frequent statements about peace and control of aggressiveness, emphasizing the avoidance of violent behavior. The *heyok'a* in contrast is given to reckless and impulsive activity. He is disruptive, noisy, obscene. He traffics in horrible substances, urinating on his clothing, throwing excrement, splashing boiling water, pretending ejaculations. He wears an enormous phallic nose and waves it about with his hands as he runs at women in the crowd. Blood, urine, feces, semen, water are equivalents to him. When one can recognize the cultural hero-shaman-priest, then his antithesis the *heyok'a* has lost his mask—he is the embodiment of the unpredictable mythological Trickster, the perpetual antagonist of the culture hero represented by the shaman.

8. The Medical System at Pine Ridge

An Oglala belief still prevalent today holds that health in the period before contact with whites was exuberant and that current diseases are the direct result of changes in lifestyle. Robert Holy Dance commented:

> The Oglala people used to live in tents [tipis]. The government forced them to live in cabins. That is what makes a health problem. All of them too crowded, at home and in school, too. All of them would get whatever disease one had. They should go back to tents the year around. One man had a lot of money and built a good house. He wouldn't live in it. He lived in a tent until he died.
>
> The government has a lot of trouble with health. I think the TB is going to come back. Because women neglect their babies. They are in a bar and don't keep them clean. *Ohe!* Put a little beer in a bottle to keep them quiet. And that's where the TB is going to come on. A baby needs a change and nobody does it. Terrible! Terrible! And those who don't take babies to a bar leave them home. All alone. And nobody to cook for them. Or the food is spoiled and they eat it anyhow. That's where your TB is going to come on again.

In the golden days, so the thought goes, game was plentiful and the people fed to repletion on good hard meat—buffalo, elk, deer, antelope. Seasonal migrations and the vigorous life were linked to procurement of large game. Plant foods and small game were supplemental, as were the maize and squash traded from the agricultural tribes. Hunting bands followed game movements, horses frequently needed fresh pasturage, and large gatherings were uncommon because they soon exhausted food and forage. The important Sun Dance, for example, required but eight days. Kin and trade visits were similarly brief. Warfare brought only a few individuals into contact, usually far from home. The lodge was portable, wastes did not accumulate, rudimentary sanitation sufficed. These patterns tended in theory to maximize isolation and ensure vitality.

As an epidemiological hypothesis, however, this is oversimple and seriously flawed by nostalgia. First, we do not know whether or to what extent traditional social structure and patterns of movement followed that reconstructed model, and how much they contributed, if they did, to aboriginal health. Second, we know next to nothing about the medical history of the plains in precontact times. The presumption is that populations were in equilibrium with disease, but there is and can be no substantial body of information about epidemic disease other than what can be inferred from the immunological unpreparedness of New World peoples to such introductions as smallpox and cholera. Third, although hunting and gathering skills allowed the evolution of complex subsistence economies, exquisitely adapted to diverse landscapes, nevertheless, seasonal and multiannual cycles must have been accompanied by population fluctuations and crises. Life could not ever have been a dependable gorge-up.

There are other difficulties with the golden-age theory. It ignores economic and cultural transformations that were occurring long before reservations came into being. Trading networks which for centuries linked the plains to other regions of the continent accommodated to new traffic in guns, furs, and metal implements. Population shifts and changes in village size and permanence followed close behind. The horse arrived on the plains in the early 1700s, and sedentary and agricultural peoples as well as nomadic bands were profoundly altered in composition and mobility thereafter. Yet more than a century was to pass before the wars with the United States brought an end to free-dom.

Disease, Diet, and Housing

Reservation life in its early, transitional, and fully developed phases saw fundamental changes in diet—the introduction of salt pork, preserved meats in barrels (sometimes already rejected by army and civilian commissaries), flour, coffee, sugar. Items abso-lutely new to Indian experience, such as tinned vegetables, lard, condiments, and cereals, needed new culinary techniques to be palatable, techniques that were slow in coming. Some items never were integrated into Oglala cuisine. As late as 1968, for one example, the roadside leading from the commodities-distri-bution warehouse was littered with discarded grapefruit. The Lakotas said they were "no good to eat, because if you bit into them they tasted terrible and if you cook them they are worse." It is notable that the availability of government-issue foods led to the virtual abandonment of materials gathered in the wild. Pack-aged rice replaced wild seeds and nuts. Canned and sugared fruits were easier to bring to the table than chokecherries and serviceberries.

Some rural people have said to me with full authority: "Be-cause we didn't pick the currants and wild plums and buffalo berries, they don't grow around here any more." But they can, in truth, be found a few yards off the roads and some few people still harvest them. Jennie Red Shirt in August 1967 had her entire family out picking chokecherries while she reduced buckets of them into pulp on a flat stone with a mano. The juicy mass was patted into small cakes, dried in the sun, stored in their hun-dreds, and made into *wójapi* in the winter. Lillian Tobacco was said to dig, peel, and braid into long bunches the wild turnip. But I never found her at home. The turnip, incidentally, lies deep in hard, dry ground and is laborious to gather. (The tubers will grow and blossom in a greenhouse but the small, gray, beanlike seeds resist germination.)

In transitional years herd beeves had been driven onto the

reservations and on issue days were turned out to be hunted down by men on horseback with some of the excitement of a buffalo run. The practice was replaced by stationary abattoirs, with an attendant loss in thrills and sanitation. Issued meat was considered "cold" or "soft," always inferior to game because it came from placid animals and transmitted their placidity to people who consumed it. Butter was judged to be a nauseating concoction that imparted a nauseating body odor. The judgment was probably well founded because rural butter making used soured cream and the product went rancid quickly.

Diets today are based on commodity food issues and resemble a generalized American poverty standard. One Lakota, for example, described his family's provisions: "We have a half sack of red beans, a half sack of white beans, and a quarter of beef tossed upon the roof of the shed. It stays frozen and out of reach of the dogs. We get through the winters fine."

The Public Health Service maintains resident clinical and research dietitians on the reservation. A comprehensive review of historical and present-day food usages and traditions may be found in *The Modern Sioux: Social Systems and Reservation Culture,* edited by Ethel Nurge.[1]

Housing has changed as radically as diet. One of the first tasks at the new agencies after the establishment of the reservations in the latter part of the nineteenth century was a census. Names were translated into English or assigned, and the enrollment lists served as the basis for issue-goods distribution. Individuals and families who had the habit of moving about or signing up at more than one agency were strongly encouraged to stay in place. Canvas replaced hide for tipi covers. Permanent, rectangular cabins were constructed as logs and sawn lumber were made available. Waste disposal remained as haphazard as before. Water was dipped from the nearest surface source. Only after a hundred years, in the 1960s, was the need for potable water met by a program of construction of small wells for isolated communities. Populations concentrated around issue points and contacts with numbers of other people became more sustained, then permanent.

The Lakotas noted "new illness, white man's illness," and ascribed it to the new diet and "houses with square corners." Contagious diseases were equated indiscriminantly with historical epidemics. It was said accusingly that "there were no catching illnesses before the whites came." Round tipis were remembered, and the idea is still expressed that they were more in harmony with nature and natural forms, with the world and the horizon, the universe, and the ceremonial objects that represent completeness and unity. Health and illness were also regularly spoken of as derived from sacred or magical power. This crucial but intangible force or process is endlessly sought in Lakota dreaming, fasting, and ceremony. It is comprehensively related to strength, health, and accomplishment, its lack with illness, weakness, and failure. An individual, for example, might gain sufficient sacred power through intensity and repetition of ritual to become himself power-filled, and thus a ritualist and healer. He might lack or lose this power and descend into illness and death. This concept of sacred power, the *wak'aŋ*, the "medicine," is central to Sioux thought in and beyond healing. An Oglala view of one devastating "white-man illness," tuberculosis, expresses a sample of attitudes about the nature of disease.

Tuberculosis became a major cause of illness and death among American Indians early in the twentieth century. It was a central concern of Dr. James R. Walker, the agency physician and a foremost student of Lakota culture, during his years on the reservation, from 1896 to 1914. The Sioux Sanatorium was established later in the century at the Rapid City Indian boarding school for the treatment and control of tuberculosis. The disease is prolonged and debilitating and requires consistent management. In the opinion of some Lakota patients and their families, this infectious disorder was evidence of a shameful character defect, a deliberate personal failure to carry out responsibilities, an unwillingness to support one's children and to meet family obligations. Individual patients were shamed and hectored in the community. Abetted by family members, patients tried to hide and deny the illness, to treat it at home, and to avoid clinic and field health workers. Once in the hospital, patients escaped as frequently as they could, making a grand adventure of it, like breaking jail. Others felt obligated to go on frequent bellicose drinking sprees "to be a man again."

These and similiar attitudes and behaviors were still common when I was asked to consult at the Sioux Sanatorium in 1967. The staff described how they were compelled to barricade themselves in the upper floors on weekends when alcoholic melees raged below. Some were displeased when I suggested police assistance was called for rather than the vague magic of a "psychiatric approach." Many individual charts at the sanatorium described patients' efforts to deal with advanced pulmonary tuberculosis through prayer, religious ecstasies, rural healers, and herbal teas. These efforts occasionally, and their secrecy and denial always, vitiated effective medical treatment of individuals and essential precautions for communities. Inevitably and unfairly the medicine men came into disrepute with physicians and nurses. The patients' yearning for cure through extrahuman means, through the ritual power derived from the supernatural and mediated by ceremonial experts, seemed to call upon another concept, an oceanic form of harmony as expressed in human life. Oglala healers use this construct to arrive at a global and expansive idea about treatment. In their discussions the ideas of causality in the Western sense become trivial. Conflict with representatives of the hospital frequently centered on this opposition.

White-Man Medicine, Indian Medicine

"White-man medicine" has been available to the Oglalas since earliest reservation days. That competent and committed physicians were assigned to the community is a part of the historical record often deliberately ignored. Medical services provided by federal agencies were at least equivalent to those of other rural areas of the nation. After 1900 the Bureau of Indian Affairs hospital at Pine Ridge and the Sioux Sanatorium for Tuberculosis at Rapid City operated on national standards and probably equaled in quality of care many other regional facilities.

In 1956 the United States Public Health Services assumed

operation of Pine Ridge medical services. Sweeping modernization of buildings, equipment, and personnel were initiated. Improvements were quickly seen in infant health and survival, tuberculosis morbidity and mortality, and infectious-disease control. The hospital achieved full approval by the Joint Commission for Hospital Accreditation, an independent national quality-surveillance body. Outpatient and hospital services and utilization increased. As part of a nationwide program for community mental health, a clinic was established at Pine Ridge and was liberally funded and staffed. Across the years a large number of talented and dedicated people have contributed to its signal success and community acceptance. Research programs in community organization, anthropology, education, psychology, and psychiatry were supported, their findings carried back to the Oglala towns by a vigorous group of nurses, social workers, physicians, and technicians. American Indian employees made up a part of the staff and contributed to the success of home-visit and outreach clinics. Research data and special studies appeared in the *Pine Ridge Research Bulletin,* which was published between 1968 and 1970. A 1969 volume by Eileen Maynard and Gayla Twiss summarized a statistical study based on interviews with all reservation families and individuals, and addressed demographic, social, economic, and psychological issues. It provided information never before available and may be unique for any comparable geographic area or tribal entity.[2]

The baseline study supported the observation that medical facilities were well used and well received by clients, but that the Oglalas wanted more and better and different ones. The high rate of medical problems was associated with poverty, education difficulties, family disorganization, a disintegrating culture, the absence of an economic base, and pervasive difficulties with role, status, and motivation. Unemployment, alcoholism, and delinquent behaviors called for sustained and organized attention. Fervent and eloquent recommendations in the Maynard and Twiss report were abundantly documented, urgently phrased, and called for the strengthening of the Oglala Sioux Health Board to engage in meaningful negotiation with the Public

Health Service. A major, adequately funded, development program was needed, with community involvement in planning and operation, and funds for long-term operation. The great number of excellent but brief programs in the past had had little surviving effect. Three areas were singled out for immediate attention: the establishment (for the first time) of a stable economic base, countering apathy and defeatism in education with an improved ethnic image and parental participation in the upgrading of schools, and encouraging leadership and political maturation through the Tribal Council. These recommendations, presumably for implementation by the same federal institutional structures pointed to as the cause of the problems in the first place, were published simultaneously with a decline in federal funding in 1970.

A public seminar was organized in 1969 by the Mental Health Clinic of the Public Health Service and the American Indian Leadership Council to consider the matters outlined above, to encourage a wider exchange of ideas, and to promote community participation. Like other such efforts conceived in great expectation of ensuing good, it did not get noticeably beyond the talking stage. The scientific papers presented meant little to the rural Oglala audience. Discussions, which were solicited, were laced with complaints, negative testimonials, and accusations. Consensus was minimal. No direction for immediate constructive action could be discerned. Soon thereafter, although not a result, came the major disruptions of Wounded Knee II. Raymond J. DeMallie reevaluated the Oglala situation almost a decade after the baseline study and its recommendations and found that little had changed.[3]

Indigenous healers were devalued by white physicians and administrators in the early reservation days. This has, in a way, come full circle. Physicians of Western medicine are now vigorously condemned by members of the activist movements. Then and now, facts were tedious and dismissive actions were more satisfying to both sides. "Town," or "white-man's," medicine was available to the Sioux in the years 1968–71 but was underutilized for reasons both rational and irrational. The modern Public

Health Hospital in Pine Ridge had skilled medical, surgical, and nursing staffs. The outpatient clinics, home-visit teams, and outreach clinics were responsive to community needs. Surrounding towns in Nebraska and South Dakota contained a spectrum of private and public medical services. But discussion about the adequacy of medical services stirred up old resentments rooted in dependency and entitlement and nurtured by long traditions of rancor and circular controversy. Piled into the mildest inquiry were economic constraints, racial fears and hatreds, political tensions and opportunism, treaty rights and violations, and the endless difficulties of good-faith communication between members of two cultures. The labor and ultimate exhaustion of many American Indians and non-Indians have gone into this morass, and sometimes seem to have sunk without a trace. The impasse has been poignantly described by Lionel H. deMontigny and Luis S. Kemnitzer.[4]

In mediation there is a maxim that resistances must be dealt with first. Beatrice Medicine has defined "from the inside" the Oglala resistance to cultural integration.[5] The reciprocal white resistance to cultural integration on the reservation has as yet no sympathetic exponent. Both bear significantly on the medical services available to the Oglalas. The gap between the two systems might have been bridged when Tribal Council offices were established in the hospital administrative wing. Although this held promise, the incumbents, both tribal and hospital, often seemed to operate in one of two unpredictable modes—cooperatively and constructively, or supervisorily and intrusively. Since tender issues of professional medical standards and native sovereignity were never far submerged, there was ample room for conflict. Rough-edged encounters that incessantly boiled up between factions and administration were nutriment to some but always destructive to patients and physicians. There was a growing list of unresolved complaints. For example, the hospital's clinic hours "didn't operate on Indian time"—and never could because staff members could not be kept on duty around the clock. Busy staff people, trying to get the job done, inadvertently violated local ideas of courtesy and pacing. Instructions and directives issued by the clinics were combed for hidden insult. Medical explanations in one language were misunderstood in the other. Patients didn't (couldn't, wouldn't) keep appointments. Country crowds thronged the hospital lobbies and toilets on weekends and during the Sun Dance and trashed the plumbing and the grounds. Such issues and many others distressed the conciliatory on both sides, while the nonconcilatory drew back into their own, muttering.

One tender issue was that the medical staff lived in a separate compound, fenced off to maintain privacy, distance, and difference. There was already an abundance of difference. The recruitment of doctors and nurses drew heavily on foreign-born and foreign-trained professionals. Many had rudimentary English. None were Lakota speakers. Invariably, hospital personnel had urban backgrounds and were unprepared to feel content in an isolated rural setting. Some felt imprisoned in the compound. Others felt imprisoned by the federal doctor-draft system. Few hospital workers made an effort at crossing the barriers and knew little about indigenous medical ideas. Social contacts were few or awkward or in time slid toward the acrimonious. In such a setting the sharing of ideas about patient care found little encouragement. A Sioux habit in painful discussions is to interrupt with a story that illustrates something or deflects conflict. In that tradition, here is a hospital chart.

A Case History of Mutism

A sixty-three-year-old woman we will call Edith was brought to the hospital because she was mute and would not eat or move. Her behavior puzzled her family and her physicians. She had no known history of mental illness, but a diagnosis was made of chronic schizophrenia. Arrangements were made to send her on to a state hospital. After all, what could be done for a chronic psychotic illness?

Sketchy biographical data were obtained from neighbors and family. She had been divorced early and reared her children by herself. As they grew older she attached herself to married offspring or near relatives. She was seldom welcome and disputes arose over who was responsible for her. Between ages forty-five and sixty she was shunted from one home to another. She was especially dependent on her daughter Darlene. She did not like Darlene's husband or Darlene's children but she clung to Darlene and her ranch house, protesting and crying over separations.

The family was restive under this determinedly dependent grandmother. The adults began to talk of leaving the reservation, whereupon Edith became even more dependent and childish. She went to a hilltop for a vision, sitting for seventy-two hours without food or water. She seemed much better thereafter. The family, encouraged, accepted a farm-labor contract at a distance. It was agreed that Edith could not go. She could not speak English. She could not use piped water, electricity, or indoor toilets. She had never been off the reservation or in a town. And besides, migrant laborers could not care for the elderly. She was left in the care of a nine-year-old grandson, who was to cook for her, and the family departed.

Edith was quiet at first, but became completely mute. She would sit on the floor and make no responses to the boy or to the neighbors. After some weeks she was taken to the hospital. There she was "difficult," mute, and motionless except when resisting examination or nursing care. Placed in a bed, she sat with legs stiffly extended, hands on lap. She tried to keep her long dress, kerchief, and moccasins. She would not touch metal or glass. Siderails were placed on the bed for her protection. Since she would not touch metal, this only made her more rigidly motionless. She urinated and defecated in a corner of the bed and soon developed bedsores. She was given antipsychotic Imipramine, Chlorpromazine, chloral hydrate, and Chloridiazepoxide. Progress awaited a nurse's realization that she could not get out of bed because she would not touch the siderails and that she didn't know how to use the bathroom. She could be shown, it was discovered, and she slowly acceded to assistance. But she never spoke. With persistent encouragement, however, she slowly gave up her phobia of the metal meal tray so that she could eat. The staff never wavered in their determination to use the standard hospital silverware and trays.

At this point a physician began to see her for twice-a-day

attempted conversations through an interpreter. She finally said that she wanted to go home. The family opposed this adamantly and demanded that she be given "shots" and be sent away for permanent state hospital care. The hospital administrative officer applied for old-age welfare and when some money from this source was assured a niece agreed to accept Edith in her home. A month after her admission, Edith left the hospital ambulatory, garrulous, and in good spirits. The chart diagnosis was "chronic schizophrenia with senility, depression, toxic brain syndrome, and drug effects."

Edith was seen at home in a series of visits and did not relapse. Neighbors and indigenous practitioners offered a different diagnosis. She was, they said, *wac'iŋk'o,* "pouting," because her daughter had gone away. They predicted she would pout again when she needed to. "Pouting is when people don't get what they want, when the situation is unbearable for them." *Wac'iŋk'o* does not appear, of course, in the hospital diagnostic handbook. Nor does pouting. But many in the Oglala community recognized it as a well-defined syndrome of anger, withdrawal, mutism, and self-destructiveness. Indigenous practitioners gave many case histories of *wac'iŋk'o* and often treated it. One must wonder how welcome *wac'iŋk'o* would have been if offered as a diagnosis at the time of Edith's admission. What other local conceptualizations lie unrecognized?

One full-blood Oglala, Stephen Gay, explaining *wac'iŋk'o,* commented: "The Standing Rock Woman—she jumped off a cliff because nobody would give her attention. She sang a song and jumped off backwards. That's pouting—*wac'iŋk'o.*" Robert Holy Dance, who was already beginning to separate himself from the world in preparation for death, said:

> *Wac'iŋk'o,* there are two or three kinds. Downhearted is a little bit different. I've been that way in my life. When a brother and sister do not hardly talk to each other, or even argue, but one goes and commits suicide, that is called *wac'iŋk'o.* Or older people get mad and go off, and commit suicide or never return.

Once at Rosebud two sisters were camping along a canyon. One of them went off and never came back. Boy, there was a manhunt that time, way down to the Sandhills, she got that far. They looked in an old house and there she was, hanging.

Another time two people [brother and sister] had a battle. The brother wanted to ride in a parade and [she] wouldn't let him borrow her horse. So he went off and shot himself. Nowadays people may argue and fight, but then they never did. But they were very touchy. There is a few people that never forget. Just like that way, yeah. They go for years and don't want to meet. It is *wac'iŋk'o*.

Pouting and downhearted are different. Downhearted affects the heart. It works into some sickness maybe in the heart or in the head or both. Red Hawk walked out of a council at Fort Laramie in 1850s, angry because someone touched the pencil. He was *wac'iŋk'o*. He never went back after that.

The nature of the Indian is much different. I was with my grandmother on my father's side. She was a Cheyenne and couldn't talk Sioux. I used to talk it as a boy but I forgot it. There was a whole bunch of people along Wolf Creek. An old man, she took care of him. Maybe her brother or something. Every morning he'd go off a little and sing: "My name is Hair Bear. I'm almost one hundred years old. I will soon now leave. I hope that you will live good," then something in Cheyenne. He was white-headed.

There used to be a woman, way down the creek. She used to sing about people who were gone. This is *wac'iŋk'o* too.

The Standing Rock Woman, she pouted. She never returned. Changed into a stone with a little dog. Women have *wac'iŋk'o* with their sickness. They used to make her [a menstruating woman] camp by herself. *Isnalat'i,* "living alone." [Men] do not go nearby or take their pipes nearby. You never go in front of a pipe. It is very strict. You don't let a woman cook, with that business [menstruation]. Indians are very touchy, even in their family. The pouting comes in there.

Both Stephen Gay and Holy Dance referred to the Standing Rock Woman. According to the "Legend of Standing Rock" in Marie McLaughlin's *Myths and Legends of the Sioux,* a Sioux married an Arikara woman and all was well until he took another wife.[6] She then became jealous and pouted, refusing to stir when the camp moved. At noon the husband, fearing she might grow desperate and kill herself, sent his two brothers back to fetch her, but she had turned into a stone and was *wak'aŋ.* The stone was thenceforth carried by the band in a special travois until it was placed on a pedestal in front of the agency building.

I am indebted to the late James H. Howard for linking this story to the prehistory of the northern plains. He was engaged in interpreting the surviving phrases of a Yanktonai Sioux winter count that extended from 1682 to 1883.[7] For the winter of 1740 the entry reads: *Wíŋyaŋ waŋ wac'iŋk'o éc'ekna íŋyaŋ ic'aǧa,* "A woman pouted and became a stone." After reading the case history of "Edith," Howard suggested: "The origin of this legend was a woman afflicted with this illness, hence we have here demonstrated historical depth for the *wac'iŋk'o* syndrome. No doubt the withdrawal, mutism, and immobility of the Arikara woman in the Standing Rock legend are what led the Dakota to believe that she actually turned to stone when they returned to look for her."

Holy Dance's Final Illness

Robert Holy Dance's experience of his final illness is another illustration of the difficulties that discolor the communications of a desperately ill patient and a competent staff, even when both are well intentioned. He became depressed after his wife's death in 1968 but he busied himself with the ritual year of mourning and seemed to recover. After the traditional feast and giveaway honoring ceremony at the anniversary of her death, however, he seemed ready to go himself. Soon he went to the hospital with a stroke and then two separate heart attacks. He began to lose sight and hearing and refused the recommended opthalmological surgery. He decided he did not want his wheelchair and abandoned it. He went on horseback once again and continued doing prophecies.

By 1971 he had been in the hospital several times but conducted his life as vigorously as before. He had episodes of severe chest pain and collapse which he hid from his family. When confronted about his secrecy he said he preferred Indian medicine. A friend conducted night sings for him. His family overrode his wishes and he was taken to a hospital, much against his will. He did not get along well with the physicians. He wanted to eat raw liver to counteract his heart "rattling" and wanted to attend *yuwipi* ceremonies. His heart "boiled" and he could not breathe in bed:

> They put ice bags on my neck but the real trouble was a lot of blood coming out my mouth. Them young doctors should be patient and not excited. I couldn't talk to them. They used three jars of that water business [intravenous fluids] and my veins swole up very big. I told them I was getting too much water and they don't pay no attention. I eat like they told me and my whole system dried up. Raw liver will regulate them two pumping places here, and I'd feel better.

At home again, he refused to recognize his increasing blindness and deafness. Instead he redefined his perceptual losses as impoverishments of the environment. Newspaper stories about the extirpation of eagles by stockmen using airplanes and shotguns, and accounts of an equine encephalitis epidemic, for example, were interwoven into the changes in himself:

> I learned a lot from going through that sickness. If I get well I'll make a good heart doctor. But so much is gone. My wife is gone, and my children. The country is changing. There ain't no birds any more. Just some little yellow ones that don't have no song. We used to have lots of birds, but they

are all gone. All killed off. The competition, everybody trying to beat everybody else. The more we go to school the worse we get. They killed all the eagles in Wyoming and that's the end of the eagles business. All the horses is getting horse disease. That's the end of the horse business. Everything is changing. I don't know if the world will last.

Holy Dance was never able to establish a comfortable relationship with his white physicians, although he often said he wanted to. And there was no relationship-between-professionals with them at all in his rural practice. He predicted his own death "during the next winter," and died at home in the coldest weather of early 1972.

9. Perspectives on Oglala Medicine

A Psychological Point of View on Ritual

Ritual is an active and reciprocal communication among individuals designed to set biological and social rhythms in motion by the manipulation of neurophysiological structures. It is imbedded in a cognitive matrix with myth, an almost infinitely diverse elaboration aimed at explanation and control of the environment. The sequences of behavior in ritual counter the arousal and responses initiated by the events of living and restore both individual and group equilibrium.[1]

A psychoanalytic interpretation of shamanism will lead us to further examination of some issues touched upon earlier in the descriptions of *yuwipi* and the Sun Dance. Robert F. Kraus notes the similarity between the world of the shaman and the world of the dream.[2] Dreams are regularly characterized by timelessness, illogical thinking, and the absence of negatives. In the working and reworking of the material the dreamer makes use of reversals, condensations, displacements, and symbolism. On the dreamer's waking, the dream is succeeded by a resynthesis, available perhaps to conscious evaluation or susceptible of interpretation. All of these features have analogues in the shaman's performance. He operates in the dark, without the usual time markers. Like the dream, his experiences seem to involve measureless time and space. His use of myth shapes the succession of events of the ceremony, his magical journeys and dangerous encounters in the world of spirits, and his return with answers and explanations for his client. For the other participants, the night-sing ceremony is the social analogue of the dream of the individual, a collective dream, an overlapping series of interpretations, participated in by all of the group. Their individual experiences include a reduction of sensory input, a drift into meditative and suggestible drowsiness or sleep, loss of a sense of time, repetitive auditory stimuli, and an induced suspension of disbelief to the extent that otherwise incredible phenomena become accepted. The shaman's skill (or the lack of it as described by Holy Dance of himself) has been elsewhere demonstrated in Apache shamans, who were seen to be adept at managing ego-controlled primary-process thought, or suspension of conscious mental activity and logical thinking, in the service of creativity and showmanship.[3]

The wish-fulfillment aspect of dreaming, and of shamanism as a cultural structure, leads one to wonder why "power" is so obsessively a feature of Sioux ceremonial life. Why does the constant emphasis on the acquisition of power pervade every fiber of Oglala ritual and myth? A model in which verbal symbols (myths) and action symbols (rituals) represent the collective Oglala dreaming state, and the expression in the dream of fundamental needs, would suggest what we already know—that in Oglala waking life power is conspicuous by its absence. Traditional concerns centered on the power to relate to nature and the cosmos, as well as the power to defeat tribal enemies. Contemporary concerns reflect as well historical conflict with white Americans. The Sioux were economically ruined and rendered politically inert after the military events of the late 1800s, and remain so within a surrounding alien culture. The recovery of autonomy has thus far eluded them. The ephemeral victories of confrontation in the 1970s are easier to understand in this context. They must have had a deeply satisfying savor to the participants, much as the entire convulsion puzzled outsiders. The power and publicity achieved at Wounded Knee II, the occupation of the deserted Alcatraz, and the other sit-ins and demonstrations were the predictable result of the profound deprivations of reservation life. Perhaps they were also the beginnings of a self-generated effort to surmount those deprivations.

A different adaptive effort was undertaken by the Utes and western Shoshones. These groups were not in the Plains culture complex, but they adopted the Sun Dance about 1890, after the collapse of their aboriginal way of life and the imposition of the stringent deprivations of reservation life, evidently in direct response to economic exploitation and political domination. They still perform it. Joseph G. Jorgensen gives us a quantitative analysis of this attempt by a powerless people to regain control of their own lives and destinies.[4] His discussion of the structure of capitalism and underdevelopment illuminates particularly well the status of other desperate American Indian groups.

The *wak'aŋ* and power are related to the psychologically interesting issue of omnipotence. We have seen the multitude of ways in which omnipotence is expressed by the rural healer, how it is a consistent quality in his functioning. Running through the descriptions of healing procedures and the commentaries, evaluations, and testimonials are the self-arrogated trappings of total competence by healers and selective inattention to their own failure. In this the healer has the implicit (and often explicit) support of his clientele. Perhaps it even originates in the client as a function of dependency. This relationship of dependency is a regular pattern between healer and client in any culture. Western literature, for example, is surfeit with idealized biographies and character studies of physicians footed in the idea that their omniscience, total competence, and dependable benevolence are inherent traits, that these can be sorted out, identified, and perhaps replicated. That the traits are the projections of the needy and supplicant laity remains unconscious; the physicians' realistic competences are obscured by the patients' needs. If doctors are not godlike, patients make them so, and insist on the distortion.

From a slightly wider perspective, the assumption of omnipotence is a response to uncertainty during professional training. In psychiatric training it is resolved as the students appreciate what they pragmatically can do against the background of what they are urged to do.[5] In less introspective specialty training its resolution is left to the leveling influences of experience. The Oglala shaman has a practical self-appraisal of what he can reasonably

undertake. His abilities are dependably supplemented by the magical omnipotence thrust upon him by his clients.

The observer of Oglala medicine and healing systems may feel that we have not yet confronted sufficiently the reasons for the dominance of magic and ritual in healing practice. After all, the close observation of natural phenomena, including disease and injury, is an acutely developed Oglala skill. Such skill is prerequisite for "scientific" thought, and it is inescapable for intelligent people to learn by trial and error the rudiments at least of empirical medicine. The Sioux were faced across millennia by the need for shrewd management of the resources available to them in a vast, meagerly productive, harsh environment. They developed an array of pragmatic behaviors, as evidenced by their survival and by the dominance they enjoyed during much of their known history. Why, then, the reliance on the imagery of the unreal, the mysteries of mythological formations? The answers lead us back to the ideas of the wak'aŋ, and to generalizations that are applicable not only to medicine and psychology but to human thought in the largest context.

David F. Aberle elegantly delineates the functions of magic, religion, charisma of healers and leaders, wak'aŋ power, and divination, all of which are the daily materials of the Oglala medicine man at work:

> Power is experienced through contact with what is unpredictable and uncontrollable, and through contact with that which or those who seem to cope with what is unpredictable and uncontrollable. Magic is a technique used to try to achieve empirical ends when empirical techniques provide inadequate prediction and control: religion is action that deals with the inevitable, unpredictable, and uncontrollable gap between the normative and the existential order; charismatic figures are unpredictable, do things other people cannot do, and force decisions in spite of lack of information: divinatory techniques use the unpredictable to predict the unpredictable. Power, prediction, and control are involved in all of these.[6]

There is a recurrent idea in anthropological writings, a bit of rusty barbed wire hidden in the brush, which holds that shamans are recovered neurotics or psychotics, or have passed through a life-threatening physical illness. Once ill themselves, the idea goes, they are able to lead others along the pathways of recovery. Some graduate student, shaking the dusty hay of old documents, will someday trace the origin of this notion. It has become solidified through repetition, and it is difficult to realize that it is an armchair idea, a too-facile explanation for men who *manipulate* illusion, delusion, and hallucination.

For example, using Siberian and arctic ethnological materials, Mircea Eliade discussed psychopathology as an initiation into and an expression of shamanic behavior. Paul Radin considered that shamans were "neurotic-epileptoid types"—a term even less informative now than when he used it, in 1957. A decade later, Julian Silverman invoked "the often noted overt similarities between the psychotic-like behaviors of marginally adjusted shamans and of acute schizophrenics," the former exhibiting "the most blatant forms of psychotic-like behaviors" and becoming "hysterical in [their] spirit possession." The "healed madman" makes no sense even when non-Western thought is forced into a narrow Western psychodiagnostic grid. In my experience, at least, the idea has no use or merit.[7]

Türüyo shamans in Surinam and Brazil, to advance my argument, are the leaders and speakers for their villages. Visitors are infrequent and often dangerous, and are conducted to the headman's hut for protracted ceremonial discourse in a special and complex language that is the particular skill of the medicine man. The ritual vocabulary is used in intertribally recognized patterns, sung or droned with wide gestures. The visitors reciprocate with similar speeches and songs that may go on for hours. The performance calls for a high level of memorization, and I thought while sitting through some of them that the speakers were extraordinarily talented, practiced, and flexible. The "recovered madman" theory seemed inapplicable then and in afterthought. On the contrary, the verbal skills indicated accomplished performers with extensive repertoires. The judgments they were called upon to make concerned trade and travel through their domains. In the recent past they have dealt with life-and-death matters with other warring tribes—hardly the task for marginal, neurotic, or deranged individuals.

Huichole shamans, for another example, are *curanderos* and *cantadores*, masters of hundreds of songs and explanations, forecasters, healers, and mediators between the Huichole *pueblitos* and the government agents and *vecinos*, the invasive Mexican farmers. Huichole shaman-leaders need to be shrewdly defensive and skilled in all manner of negotiation, and powerful enough within the tribal politics to keep the impulsive and often homicidal young men in check. Peter T. Furst has described the enormous poetic vocabularies of the Huichole and Yakut shamans, which have been estimated to contain twelve thousand words, comparable to the lexicon of a member of the European-American intellectual or literary elite, and, one supposes, to the Celtic bards of prehistory. The average Caucasian high school graduate's daily-use vocabulary, by comparison, is on the order of fifteen hundred words.[8]

Modern Changes in Oglala Ritual

Some traditional Sioux medicine men have altered their practices to conform to changing political climates, economic pressures, and evolving ideas about religion. Some have been able to develop political careers both on and off the reservation. Others have added peyote ritual to their repertoire to treat alcoholism, anomie, depression, and loss. Substantial aspects of Christian services, although explicitly rejected, have been interwoven into Oglala ceremonial. Healers have in some instances become the reservation equivalents of pastoral counselors.

In the 1970s the American Indian Movement (AIM) adopted confrontational methods, challenging and provoking the Tribal Council, tribal and off-reservation police, the Bureau of Indian Affairs, and any other authority or institution careless enough to attempt drawing limits. Bellicose racism, demonstrations, vandalism, and highly emotional pushing against any aspect of the "establishment" were encouraged. The publicity boiling up around every incident led inevitably to the tragicomic standoff at Wounded Knee in 1973. The inflammatory behavior and wild responses of both sides brought honor to none. The resolution of that affair, insofar as it has been resolved even yet, owed much to the mediational skills of Frank Fools Crow. He had the stature to represent AIM in discussions with federal negotiators, maintained his own independence and integrity in the process, and gained national recognition as an Oglala political and religious leader.

A dispassionate assessment of the Red Power movement and AIM is perhaps too much to hope for, for years to come. Atrocity stories still cloud the air. The displays of mindlessly brutal self-interest by the power seekers and their adversaries, the journalistic accounts of deception and murder, allegations of kidnapping and torture, the excited demands for justice from both white and Indian communities, the accidents and destruction, the lasting interracial fearfulness and suspicion, the dangerousness of travel on the reservation, the extirpation of tourism, the loss of many old friendships, the taking of sides by partly informed but wildly active off-reservation groups, all suggest an overwhelmingly negative ledger balance. The Sioux themselves will have to come to the ultimate evaluation. What is clear is that medicine men could and did take responsible public roles. Positions of leadership and influence are, as a positive development, more open to them than before.

Sioux Religion itself is in process of self-definition. It exists today in an accretionary mode. Ideas, rites, attitudes, and taboos are being added from diverse sources. One of its more thoughtful proponents moved, during the years I knew him, from a tolerant ecumenical point of view toward greater and greater asceticism. Taboos were multiplied as his belief system matured. He began to discourage white observers at ceremonies. He urged the avoidance of towns, automobiles, metal, and glass. He discouraged the use of hospitals and white physicians (at the same time that a severe abdominal disorder forced him to use them himself). He spoke against white-style funerals and advocated the supervision of burials and civil ceremonies by medicine men. A number of people interested in the strengthening of native American ritual systems turned to him for leadership.

I was invited to attend a wedding at his remote cabin. Before dawn a crowd gathered around a sweat-lodge fire. The medicine man went through the *inipi* and a pipe ceremony. After he dressed, the couple presented themselves as if at a church wedding, with a best man and bridesmaid. After admonitory and instructional prayers the groom placed a ring on the bride's finger. Blessings were bestowed on the couple and on the congregation. Long exhortations in ritual Lakota were given by several elders. Throughout, the medicine man conducted the proceedings much as a town minister or justice of the peace might have done. When the wedding was declared completed, a feast, water ceremony, and pipe ceremony followed. At about noon the congregation gathered up the remnants of the feast and began to disperse. The couple was presented with a hand-drawn certificate, complete with scrolls and legalistic language, declaring the marriage. An observer would be hard put to find vestiges of prereservation traditions in this new process, and might remark about the conspicuous absence of family members and gift exchanges.

The revitalized Sioux Religion has attracted wide attention. Off-reservation candidates for political office commonly exploit Oglala celebrations, seeking publicity and photographs for use in county, state, and national campaigns. These persons are wont to emphasize distant or fictitious tribal connections or to associate themselves with local programs or aspirations. Some are so transparently self-seeking as to leave their Sioux auditors grinning. Others, more genuine, nevertheless exert no discernible effect on local issues and problems. One perennial office seeker in another county appeared every year at the Sun Dance. He would reach for the microphone to speak about his war record, his speeches relying heavily on repetition and tones of unrelenting outrage:

I am here today because I believe in the great Sioux Nation. Also I want to publicly shame the Catholics for having

Mass [at the arena], for interfering with the Sun Dance. I'm the only one being pierced today, because of the interference. [Actually, he was not pierced. The piercing of the other candidates had taken place the day before.] I have the spirit of Black Elk, the holy man, who was my personal family friend. I have his pipe that has not been smoked in twenty years. I am a lawyer, and I say get off our backs or I will get on your back. That's why I'm here today, because of Catholic interference. Because I have Black Elk's pipe that hasn't been smoked since the great prophet died. Twenty years ago or so. And I have the great man Frank Andrew Fools Crow. I flew seventy missions in the war, thirty-five flights out and thirty-five back.

Perspectives on Oglala Medicine Men

The Sioux medicine man provides instruction and direction to his rural clients. In Western medical idiom he gives primary care for chronic and acute diseases. He evaluates advice and treatment given elsewhere. He has strong influence in supporting or opposing what the patient or family is told at the clinic or hospital, and in affirming, encouraging, questioning, or particularizing a given therapeutic regimen. With a shrewd attentiveness to reservation news and gossip the Sioux ritualist is a social mediator. He is able to defuse conflicts, to dispense conventional wisdom, to counsel caution, and to suggest action. The borrower who cannot dispose of some item of property and the victim who wants it back are brought together in some semblance of anonymity so that nobody loses dignity.

In his repetition of traditional Sioux themes and values the medicine man reaffirms and strengthens tribal identity. The recounting of myth and song, repeating of testimonials, emphasizing of the unity of the living with the departed dead and the historical heroes, all forge stronger links among the participants and help them take pride in their differentiation from the off-reservation culture. The night-sing ritual is wilderness theater, rural music, archaic poetry. As drama it attracts the inhabitant and outlander. Very few people in the vicinity of a good sing fail to sit in. The conjure artist, the illusionist, the serious poet and actor find their participant roles. The storyteller has audience and opportunity for well-known themes. The liturgist and the singers and drummers are in regular demand. The variations in ritual give scope to the creativity of the ritual leader, soon reflected in his fame and drawing power, public critiques, and the carping comments of competitors. The nighttime entertainment of *yuwipi* meetings, especially in the preservation of old and valued themes, resembles the ancient Cornish ordinalia, the medieval morality play, and the endlessly restated but never-changing cowboy movie. Night sings develop to the full the fine art of repetition.

The medicine man gives form and meaning to human agonies. He explains the world in his own terms. He defines and labels problems in familiar and ritual language. He underscores the comprehensiveness of his understandings. He is careful to preserve his naming prerogatives and by magical extension he asserts his power over the named objects. That he can assert this power in an ambiance of drama and share it with the tutelary spirits who are his helpers is a measure of his skill in addressing the archaic elements in human thinking, in establishing in the minds of his clients a plausible connection and identification between word and object and between word and deed. The healer names the problems and persistently seeks consensual meanings. He assigns blame and offers causal explanations that make sense in his culture. His comments are firm, confident, authoritative, autocratic. His explanations are not weighed for correctness but are accepted as oracular verbal productions. It is enough that they are organizing, reassuring, and comforting, even when they might seem to some to be irrelevant or banal.

The medicine man is an antidemonic leader. He is the formulator and teacher of the old religion and creator of the new. His ritual is carefully planned and presented. He brings an immediacy of experience with spiritual powers and the gods themselves. His multiple connections with the world above and the world below have importance to the demoralized patient frightened of the narrow grave. His symbolic representations of the universe and time emphasize their circular, ever-beginning, never-ending nature, transcending conflict and duality. He leads the thoughts of his celebrants to the ultimate and the origins, to the beginnings of knowledge, to a new perspective of Death and his motleys.

The Teton Sioux healer pays no attention to allopathic-homeopathic quarrels, to cellular physiology, germ theory, bio-chemical dynamics, molecular disturbance, or other issues of the white man's medical theory. Instead, he emphasizes his special status as an intermediary with the beings beyond knowing. He ascribes therapeutic efficacy to his supernatural helpers, to his knowledge of legend and myth, and to the strengthening of tribal identity. He participates in the ubiquitous search for personal power, that generalization which embraces health, prosperity, and mastery. He knows that his search permeates healing as well as life's other preoccupations.

The healer focuses on individuals as they are related to the group rather than on symptom, sign, disease, or diagnosis. He has a rich knowledge of his community and of family relationships and interactions. He has experimental as well as intuitive understandings of his patients' needs, and he often succeeds in recognizing unspoken wishes and expectations. The medicine man has little interest in causality, linear or multifactorial. He is impatient with sequential uncertainties. He stands upon his courage to affirm that healing will occur, and he endures as an institution in a culture that still needs him.

The ceremonies of the medicine men have been recounted here in some detail in an effort to communicate the slow rhythms of preparation and practice and the essential psychic conditioning of healer and client for the ritual itself. Preliminary arrangements may seem vague, protracted, contradictory, and undependable to non-Indian minds. They are also effectively selective of good clients and good problems, like the waiting lists of Western clinics that sometimes achieve inadvertent cures by similar time-consuming maneuvers. The long waits, the careful assessment of the patient, the need sometimes for repeated supplications, the difficulty of getting a healing session scheduled can be used to discourage the ambivalent patient and hold off an unwanted client (and the note maker). One reader of my notes felt that the reluctance of the ceremonialists to reveal themselves was more evident than I realized, but it is important, too, to recognize that my more hurried "let's do it now" was breaking against a more casual "all in good time" of rural as well as aboriginal pacing.

To the patient, all this serves to contribute to a growing implicit contract and obligation on both sides of the negotiation. The establishment of the fee, and associated costs, strengthen the contract further. The cost is sometimes high or very high in terms of the financial resources of the suppliant. The preparations asked are not trivial. Consider the time and effort necessary to prepare 405 individual tobacco-offering pouches, a day or more perhaps; and consider the personal experience of extended periods of imposed fasting, celibacy, avoidance acts and avoidance thinking, and sacrifices.

The meticulousness of instruction given to the client, the importance of every act and sequence, focus attention more and more closely and contribute to the development of altered states of awareness. The skillful use of boredom, discomfort, heat, cold, repetition, sensory overload in some modalities, and deprivation in others leads step by step to more or less profoundly experienced hypnotic states including trance and sleep. Concomitantly, there comes to be a suspension of critical judgment and of reality testing, revealed in the bemused wonderings of clients after a prolonged ritual and in the attempts at verbal review and reintegration by the participants in the hours and days after a night sing.

The intensity of the Sioux healing experience develops from the long, drawn-out ritual itself, but the intensity of the relationship with the leader is also important. The medicine man is, ambivalently, a figure of authority and awe, beyond skepticism and criticism. He is a master of procedure and a sage omnipotent. He is, furthermore, in league with powers even more awesomely omniscient and omnipotent than himself. The other side of the ambivalence appears in the off-stage gossip and derogation that seems to be an inescapable burden of healers. The patients, in their regressed surrender of autonomy and initiative, may hope that previously experienced benefits of submission will be repeated. They are reintroduced to the lost times of childhood when dream, fantasy, and reality were intermingled. Every moment, every symbolic act, every gesture with the sacred objects focuses attention on the shaman's ability to evoke an extraordinary experience. His pronouncements have the ring of universal truth.

The carefully nurtured concentration of his client's attention, dependency, and regression suggest the office techniques of the psychotherapist. The medicine man's "spirit advice," carefully formulated and carefully stated in the presence of a circle of helpers-in-ritual and beneficiaries-of-ritual, allows a comparison with the interpretations of a group therapist. The phrases of both authorities are open to emendation or restatement as the process goes on. Both attempt an integration of observation and intuition and a summary of the matters at hand in a form both individual and generalizable. The statement, restatement, and sequential clarification of the issues lead onward to reliving and abreaction, or release through recall. The rituals facilitate a benevolent community participation in the individual's pain and problem and concomitantly encourage the individual's involvement in community concerns, with a therapeutic influence on his or her alienation and narcissism. The intensity of the emotional participation that can evolve in either a night sing or a group therapy session requires a structured recovery mechanism, an after-group review, a decathecting, a social hour or a feast, a return to the present, which is now transformed. The after-group review and decathexis of the psychological work in the interest of going-on-in-reality takes various forms. In Sioux communities it is a feast as meticulously ritualized as a night sing. Detailed comparisons of shamanistic medicine and group psychotherapy are possible, and Donald Sandner gives a comparable evaluation of the psychoanalysis of ritual in his study of Navajo purification ritual and symbol manipulations.[9]

This description of Oglala medicine men reveals the variety and scope of their professional efforts. They present a surprisingly broad array of highly elaborated solutions to the problems brought to them as they address the individual, group, and community issues that concern their clients. The Oglalas, once nomadic hunters but now a sedentary rural people, have constructed many named healing procedures, each rooted in a common matrix of legend, tradition, and ceremony. None of the healing procedures exists as an isolated formulation. Each ritual carries within itself a review and reintegration of Oglala symbolic forms and a persevering emphasis on tribal identity.

The origins of Sioux healing procedures are lost in prehistory. Bear medicine seems to have been particularly developed and practiced by warriors to meet the problems of wounds and wound infections. Bear doctors have almost disappeared since battle wounds were replaced by reservation hazards. *Yuwipi* may be its direct or indirect replacement. There have been major changes in the *heyok'a* society from a warrior group to anonymous masked, ritual clowns. The Horse Dance, Weasel medicine, and Ghost medicine were rarely seen in the late 1900s. Catch-the-stone seems to be a traditional but only recently reported variant procedure. Peyotism and the Native American Church are late developments, as are fundamentalist Christian healing ideas and Alcoholic Anonymous in its distinctively Oglala forms. Herbalism is presumed to be ancient in most culture groups. Oglala *p'ejuta* herbalism is based in ritual rather than in pharmacognosy.

The *Menagiana* of 1690 referred to European medicine as "the art of keeping a patient quiet with frivolous explanations and amusing him with remedies good or bad until nature kills him or cures him."[10] Such cynicism has no counterpart in the efforts of the Oglala healers. Rather, the psychodynamics of the interchange between healer and client bear importantly on the consensus of efficacy. Healer and client undertake a culturally sanctioned interaction based on a complex structure of mutual belief which has explanatory powers for both. The intermediate symbolic objects, rituals, and medicaments proceed in such autonomous directions that "results" are almost meaningless on any but subjective terms. In the final analysis, the authority and prestige of the healer, and the regard in which he is held by patients, are commensurate with his ability to absorb and neutralize anxiety, not only the anxiety of the individuals but also that of the community in which they live.

Bibliographical Notes

This bibliographical essay will serve as a guide to the literature on Sioux ritual and healing practices. It is a large landscape, to be sure, and the reader who feels rudely abandoned at its periphery may welcome having a few major landmarks pointed out.

For the Oglalas and the Teton Sioux in general the original and irreplaceable data on traditional religion begin with James Owen Dorsey's "A Study of Siouan Cults" (1894) and James R. Walker's "The Sun Dance and Other Ceremonies of the Oglala Division of the Teton Dakota" (1917). Other basic descriptions are found in Curtis, *The North American Indian,* vol. 3 (1908), and Frances Densmore, *Teton Sioux Music* (1918). A bibliographical survey appears in Raymond J. DeMallie and Douglas R. Parks, eds., *Sioux Indian Religion* (1987:217–25).

Different and invaluable information is found in Mooney's "The Ghost-Dance Religion and the Sioux Outbreak of 1890" (1896). He describes what began as a revivalist movement and became an irresistible surge of hope wedded with conviction. It ended, predictably, in repression and the so-called Sioux outbreak of 1890. Mooney's detailed observations were among the first to illuminate the mechanisms of an attempted religious solution of desperate social realities. The Ghost Dance was a major event in the history of the Sioux people. Some other useful accounts are Raymond J. DeMallie, "The Lakota Ghost Dance" (1982); Weston La Barre, *The Ghost Dance* (1970); and Omer Stewart, "The Ghost Dance" (1980).

John G. Neihardt's *Black Elk Speaks* (1932) presents the philosophy of an Oglala holy man and was Neihardt's literary masterpiece. The book aroused a popular interest that still continues. Together with Joseph Epes Brown's *The Sacred Pipe* (1953), which continues Black Elk's account of Oglala rituals, it has generated a substantial popular following and a derivative literature that I will not attempt to review. The original transcripts of Neihardt's conversations with Black Elk are published as *The Sixth Grandfather: Black Elk's Teachings Given to John G. Neihardt,* edited by Raymond J. DeMallie (1984).

Stephen E. Feraca's *Wakinyan: Contemporary Teton Dakota Religion* (1963) is an excellent study that long served me as a handbook. It was followed by a cluster of more recent books, of great breadth and detail. William K. Powers contributed *Oglala Religion* (1977), *Yuwipi: Vision and Experience in Oglala Ritual* (1982), and *Sacred Language: The Nature of Supernatural Discourse in Lakota* (1986). Scholarly works were produced by Raymond J. DeMallie and his coeditors: *Lakota Belief and Ritual* (papers by Dr. James R. Walker), with Elaine A. Jahner (1980), and *Sioux Indian Religion* with Douglas R. Parks (1987).

The nature of the *wak'aŋ* is insightfully discussed in DeMallie and Robert H. Lavenda in "*Wakan*: Plains Siouan Concepts of Power" (1977:153–65). The reader may wish to turn to an extensive literature for its further application in Teton culture, not to mention two thousand years of Christian commentary on analogous ideas. One should see especially Walker's "Outline of Oglala Mythology" in *Lakota Belief and Ritual* (1980:50–54); Brown's *The Sacred Pipe* (1953:3–4); Powers's *Oglala Religion* (1977:200–201); and DeMallie and Parks's *Sioux Indian Religion* (1987:25–44). If one can abide the author's persistently rejective tone, Powers's *Sacred Language* (1986:11–28, 109–26) is also helpful.

The historical *haŋblec'eya* is described in DeMallie, *The Sixth Grandfather* (1984:111–42); Walker, *Lakota Belief and Ritual* (1980:55, 57, 61, 129–35, 150–53); and Brown, *The Sacred Pipe* (1953:44–66). For the modern vision quest, see Feraca, *Wakinyan* (1963:20–25) and Powers, *Oglala Religion* (1977:61–63, 91–139) and *Yuwipi* (1982:48–65, 91–93). Stuart W. Conner, "The

Archeology of the Crow Indian Vision Quest" (1984) investi-
gates the archeology of the vision quest structures of the Crow
Indians, and gives interview accounts of vision seeking.

The Sun Dance has frequently been described, in part because
of its public nature and in part because it posed a challenge in
interpretation. These studies begin with Alice C. Fletcher's "The
Sun Dance of the Ogalalla Sioux" (1883) and Frederick Schwatka's "The Sun-Dance of the Sioux" (1890). Walker's writings
("The Sun Dance and Other Ceremonies of the Oglala Division
of the Teton Dakota," 1917) are classic and beautiful and are now
supplemented by his edited papers (*Lakota Belief and Ritual,*
1980). Good descriptions are also found in Dorsey, "A Study of
Siouan Cults" (1894); Brown, *The Sacred Pipe* (1953); Feraca,
Wakinyan (1963); Ethel Nurge, *The Modern Sioux* (1970), Zimmerly, "On Being an Ascetic" (1969), and Powers, *Oglala Religion* (1977). The Sun Dances of the years covered by this mono-
graph were summarized in Thomas H. Lewis's "The Oglala
(Teton-Dakota) Sundance" (1972).

Many Plains tribes other than the Oglalas conducted Sun
Dances in their own styles and variations. The complexities of
large and small differences have contributed confusion to the
understanding of core elements. An excellent guide is Joseph G.
Jorgensen's sociological analysis of the Ute and Shoshone Sun
Dance, *The Sun Dance Religion* (1972). It is directly applicable to
the functional components of the Oglala rite.

For many it will suffice to observe or participate in the splen-
dor of the Teton dance ceremonies with these works as reference,
while others may wish to take a long step beyond. For these,
Edmund Leach's analyses of thought and communication (*Culture and Communication,* 1976) are a lasting intellectual feast.
James W. Fernandez's "Analysis of Ritual" (1973) and "The
Mission of Metaphor in Expressive Culture" (1974) and Roger
Caillois' *L'Homme et le sacré* (1950) are also concerned with the
meaning in ritual. D'Aquili et al. (*The Spectrum of Ritual,* 1979)
approach ceremony as a genetic and biological phenomenon and
examine its neurobiology, evolution, comparative ethnology, cy-
bernetics and coding, cognition, and structural transformations.

Fred W. Voget, in *The Shoshone-Crow Sun Dance* (1984) describes the analogous Shoshone-Crow ceremony.

The siftings of early writings on *yuwipi* are incomplete. As a night ritual it may have been overlooked, and terms denoting it may have changed. Still, neither Clark Wissler, "Societies and Ceremonial Associations in the Oglala Division of the Teton-Dakota" (1912); Walker, "The Sun Dance and Other Ceremonies of the Oglala Division of the Teton Dakota" (1917); nor Brown, *The Sacred Pipe* (1953) mentions it, although it is unlikely that they should have been unaware of it. It is not a reservation development certainly; Prince Maximilian of Wied encountered a celebrated Cree medicine man or conjurer in 1833 and described him in detail (Thomas and Ronnefeldt, *People of the First Man*, 1976:158). Called Mahsette-Kuinah, "The Rattler," this medicine man used tied-shaman and shaking-tent procedures, the audience remaining outside the tent. After a prolonged sound of drums, the tent began to tremble and the voices of bears, buffalo, and other animals were heard. The shaman later interpreted the message from a spirit he had questioned. He was much respected, and his prophetic successes were much quoted, Maxmillian says, by Canadians and Indians alike. A description of a *yuwipi* equivalent among the Gros Ventres appears in Alfred L. Kroeber's "Ethnology of the Gros Ventre" (1907).

Luis Kemnitzer ("Cultural Provenience of Objects Used in *Yuwipi*," 1970, and "Structure, Context, and Cultural Meaning of Yuwipi," 1976) is a profound student of *yuwipi*. Powers, *Yuwipi* (1982) and Feraca, *Wakinyan* (1963) give detailed accounts and Elizabeth S. Grobsmith, "*Wakunza*: Uses of *Yuwipi* Medicine Power in Contemporary Teton Dakota Culture" (1974) presents a valuable recent evaluation.

Covering the period during which the material for my study was being gathered, John Fire (Lame Deer) and Richard Erdoes produced a journalistic account of a Teton medicine man (*Lame Deer, Seeker of Visions*, 1972). Thomas Mails's *Fools Crow* (1979) is the life story of another leading medicine man, and Mails's *Sundancing at Rosebud and Pine Ridge* (1978) includes interviews with Fools Crow and others.

Robert F. Kraus, "A Psychoanalytic Interpretation of Shamanism" (1972) describes shamanic ritual in psychoanalytic terms as the social analogue of the dream. My understanding of the dynamics of ritual was much enriched by Donald Sandner's studies of Navajo nine-day ceremonies (*Navaho Symbols of Healing*, 1979). Sandner also examines other preliterate symbolic healing systems and compares them with modern psychotherapy and medical practice.

Notes

INTRODUCTION
1. Furst (1972), Meyerhoff (1974), Schultes (1972), La Barre (1975), Lumholtz (1902), Sahagun (1950–69 [1560]).

CHAPTER 1
1. Dlugokinski and Kramer (1974).

CHAPTER 2
1. See Bergman (1973).
2. Robicsek (1978).
3. See especially Smith (1967).

CHAPTER 3
1. Walker (1917).

CHAPTER 4
1. Hurt and Howard (1952), Hurt (1960; 1961), Feraca (1961; 1963), Fugle (1966).
2. Walker (1980), Powers (1977, 1982). On the differentiation of the Eagle power ceremony from *yuwipi* see Feraca (1962).
3. Lewis (1980b).

CHAPTER 5
1. Ewers (1982:36–45).

2. Ewers (1968:131–45), Wissler (1912:88–90), Denig (1961:537–38).
3. Densmore (1918:95), Walker (1980:136, 157–59).
4. Walker (1980:91–93), Powers (1977:58).
5. Fire (1972:153–54), Feraca (1963:40).
6. Neihardt (1932:166–80), De-Mallie (1984:215–26), Feraca (1963:43–44).
7. Powers (1977), Walker (1980:51, 71), Hurt (1960).
8. Synan (1971), Hollenweyer (1972).
9. Feraca (1963:25).

CHAPTER 6
1. Buechel (1970:120).
2. Buechel (1970:123).
3. Buechel (1970:469).
4. Buechel (1970:183).
5. Buechel (1970:200).
6. Buechel (1970:520).
7. Walker (1980:93).
8. Grinnell (1923 2:182–83), Rydberg (1965:590), McDougall and Baggley (1956:114), Lowie (1935:63).

9. Buechel (1970), Rogers (1980), Feraca (1963:58–65).

CHAPTER 7
1. Opler (1938), Parsons and Beals (1934), Wallis (1947:111), Dorsey (1894).
2. Walker (1980:14, 155–57, 277–80), Lowie (1913b:207–11), DeMallie (1984:232–35).
3. Gilmore in Grinnell (1923 2:205n).
4. Smith (1967:15).
5. Howard (1977:161).
6. Caillot (1950:205), Makarius (1970).

CHAPTER 8
1. Nurge (1970).
2. Maynard and Twiss (1969).
3. DeMallie (1978).
4. deMontigny (1969), Kemnitzer (1969b).
5. Medicine (1981).
6. McLaughlin (1916:40–41).
7. James H. Howard (personal letter, 28 August 1975). The Yanktonai winter count was published in Howard (1976).

CHAPTER 9
1. Descriptions of neurophysiological mechanisms underlying ritual have been drawn together by D'Aquili et al. (1979) and are useful in the understanding of shamanic medicine. Their essays emerge from an enormous literature on comparative ethology and central nervous system anatomy.
2. Kraus (1972).
3. Boyer et al. (1964, 1985).
4. Jorgensen (1972).
5. Lewin (1958) and Sharaf and Levinson (1964) concluded from observation of psychiatric residents in training that omniscience and omnipotence are inevitable reaction-formations against uncertainty and are analyzable aspects of the learning process.
6. Aberle (1966b:229).
7. Eliade (1951:23–24), Radin (1957:131), Silverman (1967:2, 5, 6).
8. Furst (1972:57–58; 1973–74).
9. Sandner (1979).
10. Strauss (1968:295).

Bibliography

Aberle, David F.
1966a The Peyote Religion among the Navaho. Chicago: Aldine Publishing Company.
1966b Religio-Magical Phenomena and Power, Prediction, and Control. Southwestern Journal of Anthropology 22:221–30.
1973 The Sun Dance and Reservation Underdevelopment: A Review Essay. Journal of Ethnic Studies 1:66–73.

Ackerkneckt, Edward H.
1942 Primitive Medicine and Culture Pattern. Bulletin of the History of Medicine 11:503–21.

Albaugh, Bernard J., and Philip O. Anderson
1974 Peyote in the Treatment of Alcoholism among American Indians. American Journal of Psychiatry 131:1247–50.

Bad Heart Bull, Amos
1967 A Pictographic History of the Oglala Sioux. Text by Helen H. Blish. Lincoln: University of Nebraska Press.

Benedict, Ruth
1922 The Vision Quest in Plains Culture. American Anthropologist 24:1–23.
1923 The Concept of the Guardian Spirit in North America. American Anthropological Association, Memoir 29.

Bergman, R. L.

1973   A School for Medicine Men. American Journal of Psychiatry 130:663–66.

Bourke, John G.

1892   The Medicine Men of the Apache. Smithsonian Institution, Bureau of American Ethnology, Annual Report 9:451–603. Washington, D.C.

Boyer, L. Bryce, George A. DeVos, and Ruth M. Boyer

1985   Crisis and Continuity in the Personality of an Apache Shaman. *In* The Psychoanalytic Study of Society: Essays in Honor of Werner Muensterberger, vol. 11, ed. L. Bryce Boyer and Simon A. Grolnick, pp. 63–113. Hillsdale, N.J.: Analytic Press.

Boyer, L. Bryce, et al.

1964   Comparisons of the Shamans and Pseudoshamans of the Apaches of the Mescalero Indian Reservation: A Rorschach Study. Journal of Projective Techniques and Personality Assessment 28:173–80.

Brown, Joseph Epes, recorder and ed.

1953   The Sacred Pipe: Black Elk's Account of the Seven Rites of the Oglala Sioux. Norman: University of Oklahoma Press. Reprint ed., New York: Penguin Books, 1971.

Buechel, Eugene, S.J.

1970   A Dictionary of the Teton Dakota Sioux Language. Edited by Paul Manhart, S.J. Pine Ridge, S.Dak.: Red Cloud Indian School.

Bushotter, George

1887–88   Lakota texts, with interlinear English translations by James Owen Dorsey. Manuscript, National Anthropological Archives, Smithsonian Institution, Washington, D.C.

Caillois, Roger

1950   L'Homme et le sacré. Paris: Gallimard.

Cohen, S.

1982   Alcohol and the Indian. Drug Abuse and Alcoholism Newsletter 11(4):1–3.

Coles, Robert

1977 Children of Crisis: Eskimos, Chicanos and Indians. Vol. 4. Boston: Little, Brown.

Conner, Stuart W.

1984 The Archeology of the Crow Indian Vision Quest. Archeology in Montana 23(3):85–127.

Cooper, John M.

1944 The Shaking Tent Rite among Plains and Forest Algonquians. Primitive Man 17:60–84.

Corlett, William Thomas

1935 The Medicine-Man of the American Indian and His Cultural Background. Springfield, Ill.: Charles C. Thomas.

Curtis, Edward S.

1908 The North American Indian. Vol. 3. Reprint ed., New York: Johnson Reprint Corp., 1970.

Cushman, Dan

1953 Stay Away, Joe: A Novel. New York: Viking Press.

D'Aquili, Eugene G., Charles D. Laughlin, Jr., and John McManus

1979 The Spectrum of Ritual: A Biogenetic Structural Analysis. New York: Columbia University Press.

DeMallie, Raymond J.

1978 Pine Ridge Economy: Cultural and Historical Perspectives. *In* American Indian Economic Development, ed. Sam Stanley, pp. 237–312. The Hague: Mouton.

1982 The Lakota Ghost Dance: An Ethnohistorical Account. Pacific Historical Review 51:385–405.

———, ed.

1984 The Sixth Grandfather: Black Elk's Teachings Given to John G. Neihardt. Lincoln: University of Nebraska Press.

———, with Robert H. Lavenda

1977 *Wakan*: Plains Siouan Concepts of Power. *In* The Anthropology of Power: Ethnographic Studies from Asia, Oceania and the New

World, ed. Richard Adams and Raymond D. Fogelson, pp. 154–66. New York: Academic Press.

————, with Douglas R. Parks, eds.

1986 Sioux Indian Religion: Tradition and Innovation. Norman: University of Oklahoma Press.

deMontigny, Lionel H.

1969 Doctor-Indian Patient Relationship. Pine Ridge Research Bulletin 8:28–39.

Denig, Edwin T.

1961 Five Indian Tribes of the Upper Missouri. Edited by John C. Ewers. Norman: University of Oklahoma Press.

Densmore, Frances

1918 Teton Sioux Music. Smithsonian Institution, Bureau of American Ethnology, Bulletin 91. Washington, D.C.: Government Printing Office.

Devereux, George

1951 Reality and Dream: Psychotherapy of a Plains Indian. New York: International Universities Press.

Dizmang, Larry H.

1967 Suicide among the Cheyenne Indians. Bulletin of Suicidology 7:8–11.

Dlugokinski, Eric L., and Lyn Kramer

1974 A System of Neglect: Indian Boarding Schools. American Journal of Psychiatry 131:670–73.

Dorsey, James Owen

1894 A Study of Siouan Cults. Smithsonian Institution, Bureau of American Ethnology, Annual Report 11:350–544. Washington, D.C.

Duffy, John

1976 The Healers: The Rise of the Medical Establishment. New York: McGraw-Hill.

Eliade, Mircea
1951 Shamanism: Archaic Techniques of Ecstasy. Princeton: Princeton University Press.

Erickson, Erik H.
1939 Observations on Sioux Education. Journal of Psychology 7:110–56.
1963 Childhood and Society. 2d ed. New York: W. W. Norton.

Ewers, John C.
1968 Indian Life on the Upper Missouri. Norman: University of Oklahoma Press.
1982 The Awesome Bear in Plains Indian Art. American Indian Art 7:36–45.

Feraca, Stephen E.
1961 The Yuwipi Cult of the Oglala and Sicangu Teton Sioux. Plains Anthropologist 6:155–63.
1962 The Teton Sioux Eagle Medicine Cult. American Indian Tradition 8:195–96.
1963 Wakinyan: Contemporary Teton Dakota Religion. Studies in Plains Anthropology and History 2. Browning, Mont.: Museum of the Plains Indian.

———, with James H. Howard
1963 The Identity and Demography of the Dakota or Sioux Tribe. Plains Anthropologist 8:80–84.

Fernandez, James W.
1973 Analysis of Ritual: Metaphoric Correspondences as the Elementary Forms. Science 182:1366.
1974 The Mission of Metaphor in Expressive Culture. Current Anthropology 15:119–45.

Fernberger, Samuel W., and Frank G. Speck
1938 Two Sioux Shields and Their Psychological Interpretation. Journal of Abnormal and Social Psychology 33:168–78.

Fire, John (Lame Deer), and Richard Erdoes
1972 Lame Deer, Seeker of Visions. New York: Simon and Schuster.

Fletcher, Alice C.

1883　The Sun Dance of the Ogalalla Sioux. Proceedings of the American Association for the Advancement of Science 31:580–84.

Frank, André G.

1967　Capitalism and Underdevelopment in Latin America: Historical Studies of Chile and Brazil. New York: Monthly Review Press.

Fugle, Eugene

1966　The Nature and Functions of the Lakota Night Cults. W. H. Over Museum, University of South Dakota, Museum News 27:1–38.

Furst, Peter T.

1972　To Find Our Life: Peyote among the Huichol Indians of Mexico. *In* Flesh of the Gods: The Ritual Use of Hallucinogens, ed. Peter T. Furst, pp. 136–184. New York: Praeger.

1973–74　The Roots and Continuities of Shamanism. *In* Stones, Bones, and Skin: Ritual and Shamanic Art. Arts Canada 20(5&6):33–60.

Glick, Leonard B.

1971　Review of *Shamanism: The Beginnings of Art* by Andreas Lommel. Current Anthropology 11:41–42.

Goldfrank, Esther S.

1943　Historic Change and Social Character: A Study of the Teton Dakota. American Anthropologist 45:67–83.

Grinnell, George Bird

1923　The Cheyenne Indians: Their History and Way of Life. 2 vols. New Haven: Yale University Press.

Grobsmith, Elizabeth S.

1974　*Wakuⁿza*: Uses of *Yuwipi* Medicine Power in Contemporary Teton Dakota Culture. Plains Anthropologist 19:129–33.

1979　The Lakhota Giveaway: A System of Social Reciprocity. Plains Anthropologist 24:123–31.

1981　The Changing Role of the Giveaway Ceremony in Contemporary Lakota Life. Plains Anthropologist 26:75–79.

Group for the Advancement of Psychiatry

1968 The Psychic Function of Religion in Mental Illness and Health. Report no. 67. New York.

Hagan, Everett E.

1962 On the Theory of Social Change: How Economic Growth Begins. A Study from the Center for International Studies, MIT. Homewood, Ill.: Dorsey Press.

Halifax, Joan

1979 Shamanic Voices: A Survey of Visionary Narrative. New York: E. P. Dutton.

Hassrick, Royal B.

1964 The Sioux: Life and Customs of a Warrior Society. Norman: University of Oklahoma Press.

Hoebel, E. Adamson

1960 The Cheyennes: Indians of the Great Plains. New York: Holt, Rinehart and Winston.

Hollenweyer, W. J.

1972 The Pentecostals: The Charismatic Movement in the Churches. Minneapolis: Augsburg.

Howard, James H.

1954 The Dakota Heyoka Cult. Scientific Monthly 78:254–58.

1961 A Note on the Dakota Water Drinking Society. American Indian Tradition 7:96.

1976 Yanktonai Ethnohistory and the John K. Bear Winter Count. Memoir 11. Plains Anthropologist 21(2).

1977 The Plains-Ojibwa or Bungi. Reprint ed., Lincoln: J&L Reprint Company. (Original ed., 1965.)

1979 Some Further Thoughts on Eastern Dakota "Clans." Ethnohistory 26:133–40.

Hsu, Francis L. K.

1961 Psychological Anthropology: Approaches to Culture and Personality. Homewood, Ill.: Dorsey Press.

Hurt, Wesley R.

1960   A Yuwipi Ceremony at Pine Ridge. Plains Anthropologist 5:48–52.

1961   A Correction on Yuwipi Color Symbolism. Plains Anthropologist 6:43.

————, and James H. Howard

1952   A Dakota Conjuring Ceremony. Southwestern Journal of Anthropology 8:286–96.

Indian, The

1970   Newsletter, American Indian Leadership Council.

Jones, David E.

1972   Sanapia: Comanche Medicine Woman. Holt, Rinehart and Winston.

Jorgensen, Joseph G.

1972   The Sun Dance Religion: Power for the Powerless. Chicago: University of Chicago Press.

Kemnitzer, Luis S.

1969a Yuwipi. Pine Ridge Research Bulletin 10:26–33.

1969b White Man's Medicine, Indian Medicine, and Indian Identity on Pine Ridge Reservation. Pine Ridge Research Bulletin 8:12–23.

1970   Cultural Provenience of Objects Used in *Yuwipi*: A Modern Teton Dakota Healing Ritual. Ethnos 35:40–75.

1976   Structure, Context, and Cultural Meaning of Yuwipi: A Modern Lakota Healing ritual. American Ethnologist 3:261–80.

Klopfer, Bruno, and L. Bryce Boyer

1961   Notes on the Personality Structure of a North American Indian Shaman: Rorschach Interpretation. Journal of Projective Techniques 25:170–78.

Kraus, Robert F.

1972   A Psychoanalytic Interpretation of Shamanism. Psychoanalytic Review 59(1):19–32.

Kroeber, Alfred L.
1907 Ethnology of the Gros Ventre. American Museum of Natural History, Anthropological Papers 1:145–281.

La Barre, Weston
1970 The Ghost Dance: The Origins of Religion. New York: Doubleday. Revised ed., New York: Delta Books, 1972.
1975 The Peyote Cult. 4th ed., enlarged. New York: Schocken Books.

Leach, Edmund
1976 Culture and Communication: The Logic by Which Symbols Are Connected. An Introduction to the Use of Structural Analysis in Social Anthropology. Cambridge: Cambridge University Press.

Lévi-Strauss, Claude
1982 The Way of the Masks. Seattle: University of Washington Press.

Lewin, Bertram D.
1958 Education or the Quest for Omniscience. Journal of American Psychoanalytic Association 6:389–412.

Lewis, Oscar
1959 Five Families: Mexican Case Studies in the Culture of Poverty. New York: Basic Books.
1961 The Children of Sánchez: Autobiography of a Mexican Family. New York: Random House.
1966 La Vida: A Puerto Rican Family in the Culture of Poverty—San Juan and New York. New York: Random House.

Lewis, Thomas H.
1968 Sun Dance, 1968. Pine Ridge Research Bulletin 5:52–64.
1970 Notes on the Heyoka, the Teton-Dakota "Contrary" Cult. Pine Ridge Research Bulletin 11:7–19.
1972 The Oglala (Teton-Dakota) Sundance: Vicissitudes of Its Structure and Function. Plains Anthropologist 17:44–49.
1973 Oglala (Sioux) Concepts of Homosexuality and the Determinants of Sexual Identification. Journal of the American Medical Association 225:312–13.
1974a The *Heyoka* Cult in Historical and Contemporary Oglala Sioux Society. Anthropos 69:17–32.

1974*b* An Indian Healer's Preventive Medicine Procedure. Hospital and Community Psychiatry 25:94–95.

1975 A Syndrome of Depression and Mutism in the Oglala Sioux. American Journal of Psychiatry 137:753–55.

1977 Therapeutic Techniques of Huichole Curanderos with a Case Report of Cross Cultural Psychotherapy (Mexico). Anthropos 72: 709–16.

1980*a* An Amazonian Drugstore: Reflections on Pharmacotherapy and Phantasy. Diogene 117:42–57.

1980*b* The Changing Practice of the Oglala Medicine Man. Plains Anthropologist 25:265–67.

1980*c* An Ethnopharmacologic Search for the Identity of *Canli Icahiye*. Plains Anthropologist 25:87–88.

1980*d* A Sioux Medicine Man Describes His Own Illness and Approaching Death. Annals of Internal Medicine 92:265–67.

1981 Phallic Masks and Fear of Sexuality. Journal of Operational Psychiatry 12:100–104.

1982 Group Therapy Techniques in Shamanistic Medicine. Journal of Group Psychotherapy, Psychodrama, and Sociometry. Spring:24–30.

1982 The Evolution of the Social Role of the Oglala *Heyoka*. Plains Anthropologist 27:249–53.

1987 The Contemporary *Yuwipi*. *In* Sioux Indian Religion: Tradition and Innovation, ed. Raymond J. DeMallie and Douglas R. Parks. Norman: University of Oklahoma Press.

Liberty, Margot

1980 The Sun Dance. *In* Anthropology on the Great Plains, ed. W. Raymond Wood and Margot Liberty, pp. 164–78. Lincoln: University of Nebraska Press.

Lowie, Robert H.

1913*a* Dance Associations of the Eastern Dakota. American Museum of Natural History, Anthropological Papers 11:101–42.

1913*b* Societies of the Crow, Hidatsa and Mandan Indians. American Museum of Natural History, Anthropological Papers 11:143–358.

1935 The Crow Indians. New York: Fararr and Rinehart.

Lumholtz, Karl S.

1900 Symbolism of the Huichol Indians. American Museum of Natural History, Memoirs vol. 3, pp. 1–228. New York.

1902 Unknown Mexico: A Record of Five Years' Exploration among the Tribes of the Western Sierra Madre. . . . 2 vols. New York: Charles Scribner's Sons.

1904 Decorative Art of the Huichol Indians. American Museum of Natural History, Memoirs vol. 3, pp. 279–327. New York.

Lynd, J. W.

1864 The Religion of the Dakotas. Minnesota Historical Society Collections 2:150–74. St. Paul, Minn. 2d ed., 1886.

McDougall, Walter B., and Herman A. Baggley

1956 The Plants of Yellowstone National Park. 2d ed. Yellowstone Park, Wyo.: Yellowstone Library and Museum Association.

Macgregor, Gordon H.

1946 Warriors without Weapons: A Study of the Society and Personality Development of the Pine Ridge Sioux. Chicago, Ill.: University of Chicago Press.

McGregor, James H.

1940 The Wounded Knee Massacre from the Viewpoint of the Sioux. Baltimore: Wirth Brothers.

McLaughlin, Marie L.

1916 Myths and Legends of the Sioux. Bismarck, N.Dak.: Bismarck Tribune Co.

Maddox, John L.

1923 The Medicine Man: A Sociological Study of the Character and Evolution of Shamanism. New York: Macmillan.

Mails, Thomas

1978 Sundancing at Rosebud and Pine Ridge. Sioux Falls: Center for Western Studies, Augustana College.

1979 Fools Crow. New York: Doubleday.

Makarius, Laura

1968 The Blacksmith's Taboos: From the Man of Iron to the Man of Blood. Diogenes 62:25–48.

1970 Ritual Clowns and Symbolical Behaviour. Diogenes 69:44–73.

Malan, Vernon D.

1958 The Dakota Indian Family: Community Studies on the Pine Ridge Reservation. Bulletin 470. Brookings, S.Dak.: Rural Sociology Department, South Dakota State College.

———, and Clinton J. Jesser

1959 The Dakota Indian Religion. Bulletin 473. Brookings, S.Dak.: Rural Sociology Department, South Dakota State College.

Maximilian, Prince of Wied

1906 Travels in the Interior of North America, 1832–1834, Part 1. *In* Early Western Travels, 1748–1846, ed. Reuben Gold Thwaites. Cleveland: Arthur H. Clark.

Maynard, Eileen, and Gayla Twiss

1969 That These People May Live: Conditions among the Oglala Sioux of the Pine Ridge Reservation. Pine Ridge, S.Dak.: Community Mental Health Program.

Medicine, Beatrice

1981 Native American Resistance to Integration: Contemporary Confrontations and Religious Revitalization. Plains Anthropologist 26:277–86.

Mekeel, H. Scudder

1936 The Economy of a Modern Teton Dakota Community. Yale University Publications in Anthropology 6. New Haven: Yale University Press.

1936 An Anthropologist's Observation on Indian Education. Progressive Education 13:151–59.

1943 A Short History of the Teton-Dakota. North Dakota Historical Quarterly 10:136–205.

Meyerhoff, Barbara G.

1970 The Deer-Maize-Peyote Symbol Complex among the Huichol Indians of Mexico. Anthropological Quarterly 43:64–78.

1974 Peyote Hunt: The Sacred Journey of the Huichol Indians. Ithaca: Cornell University Press.

Mindell, C., and P. Stuart

1968 Suicide and Self-Destructive Behavior in the Oglala Sioux: Some Clinical Aspects and Community Approaches. Pine Ridge Research Bulletin 1:14–23.

Mooney, James

1896 The Ghost-Dance Religion and the Sioux Outbreak of 1890. Smithsonian Institution, Bureau of American Ethology, Annual Report 14, pt. 2. Abridged, with an introduction by Anthony F. C. Wallace. Chicago: University of Chicago Press, 1965.

Morgan, George R.

n.d. Anthropological Study of Peyote. Typescript, Chadron State College, Chadron, Nebr.

n.d. Half-Moon Peyotists of the Pine Ridge Indian Reservation. Typescript, Chadron State College, Chadron, Nebr.

Muensterberger, Werner, and Sidney Axelrad et al., eds.

1960–85 The Psychological Study of Society. 11 vols. Hillsdale, N.J.: Analytic Press.

Neihardt, John G.

1932 Black Elk Speaks: Being the Life Story of a Holy Man of the Ogalala Sioux. New York: William Morrow. New ed., Lincoln: University of Nebraska Press, 1972, 1979.

Nurge, Ethel, ed.

1970 The Modern Sioux: Social Systems and Reservation Culture. Lincoln: University of Nebraska Press.

Oglala War Cry, The

1970 Newspaper published by the Oglala Sioux Tribe. Pine Ridge, S.Dak.

Opler, M. E.

1936 Some Points of Comparison and Contrast between the Treatment of Functional Disorders by Apache Shamans and Modern Psychiatric Practice. American Journal of Psychiatry 92:1371–87.

Paige, Harry W.

1970 Songs of the Teton Sioux. Los Angeles: Westernlore Press.

Parsons, Elsie Clews, and Ralph L. Beals

1934 The Sacred Clowns of the Pueblo and Mayo-Yaqui Indians. American Anthropologist 36:491–514.

Powell, Peter John

1969 Sweet Medicine: The Continuing Role of the Sacred Arrows, the Sun Dance, and the Sacred Buffalo Hat in Northern Cheyenne History. 2 volumes. Norman: University of Oklahoma Press.

Powers, William K.

1977 Oglala Religion. Lincoln: University of Nebraska Press.
1982 Yuwipi: Vision and Experience in Oglala Ritual. Lincoln: University of Nebraska Press.
1986 Sacred Language: The Nature of Supernatural Discourse in Lakota. Norman: University of Oklahoma Press.

Radin, Paul

1957 Primitive Man as Philosopher. Enlarged ed., New York: Dover Publications. (Original ed., 1927.)

Ray, Verne F.

1941 Historic Background of the Conjuring Complex in the Plateau and the Plains. In Language, Culture, and Personality: Essays in Memory of Edward Sapir. Ed. Leslie Spier et al., pp. 204–16. Menasha, Wis.: Sapir Memorial Publication Fund.

Resnik, H.L.P., and L. H. Dizmang

1971 Observations on Suicidal Behavior among American Indians. American Journal of Psychiatry 127(7):58–63.

Riggs, Stephen R.
1869 Taȟ-koo Wa-kaṅ; or, The Gospel among the Dakotas. Boston: Congregational Publishing Society.

Robicsek, Francis
1978 The Smoking Gods: Tobacco in Maya Art, History, and Religion. Norman: University of Oklahoma Press.

Rogers, Dilwyn J.
1980 Lakota Names and Traditional Uses of Native Plants by Sicangu (Brule) People in the Rosebud Area, South Dakota. St. Francis, S.Dak.: Rosebud Educational Society.

Ruby, Robert H.
1955 The Oglala Sioux: Warriors in Transition. New York: Vantage Press.
1966 Yuwipi: Ancient Rite of the Sioux. Montana: The Magazine of Western History 16:74–79.

Rydberg, Per Axel
1965 Flora of the Prairies and Plains of Central North America. New York: Hafner Publishing. (Original ed., 1932.)

Sahagún, Bernardino de
1950–69 General History of the Things of New Spain: Florentine Codex Translated from the Aztec into English, with Notes and Illustrations. Translated and edited by Arthur J. O. Anderson and Charles E. Dibble, Santa Fe, N.M.: School of American Research.

Sandner, Donald
1979 Navaho Symbols of Healing. New York: Harcourt, Brace, Jovanovich.

Sandoz, Mari
1961 These Were the Sioux. New York: Hastings House.

Schultes, Richard Evans
1972 An Overview of Hallucinogens in the Western Hemisphere. *In* Flesh of the Gods: The Ritual Use of Hallucinogens, ed. Peter T. Furst, pp. 3–54. New York: Praeger.

Schwatka, Fredrick

1889–90 The Sun-Dance of the Sioux. Century Magazine 39:753–59.

Shannon County News

1968 Weekly newspaper. Martin, South Dakota.

Sharaf, Myron R., and Daniel J. Levinson

1964 The Quest for Omnipotence in Professional Training: The Case of the Psychiatric Resident. Psychiatry 27:135–49.

Shimkin, Demitri B.

1953 The Wind River Shoshone Sun Dance. Smithsonian Institution, Bureau of American Ethnology, Bulletin 51:397–484. Washington, D.C.: Government Printing Office.

Silverman, Julian

1967 Shamans and Acute Schizophrenia. American Anthropologist 69:21–31.

Slotkin, James S.

1956 The Peyote Religion: A Study in Indian-White Relations. Glencoe, Ill.: Free Press.

Smith, J. L.

1967 A Short History of the Sacred Calf Pipe of the Teton Dakota. W. H. Over Museum, University of South Dakota, Museum News 28(7–8):1–37.

Spier, Leslie

1925 An Analysis of Plains Indian Parfleche Decoration. University of Washington, Publications in Anthropology 1(3). Seattle, Wash.

Stewart, Omer C.

1980 The Ghost Dance. In Anthropology on the Great Plains, ed. W. Raymond Wood and Margot Liberty, pp. 179–87. Lincoln: University of Nebraska Press.

Strauss, M. B., ed.

1968 Familiar Medical Quotations. Boston: Little, Brown.

Synan, Vinson

1971 The Holiness Pentecostal Movement in the United States. Grand Rapids, Mich.: William R. Eerdmans.

Thomas, David, and Karen Ronnefeldt, eds.

1976 People of the First Man, Life among the Plains Indians in Their Final Days of Glory: The Firsthand Account of Prince Maximilian's Expedition up the Missouri River, 1833–34. New York: E. P. Dutton.

Voget, Fred W.

1953 Current Trends in the Wind River Shoshone Sun Dance. Smithsonian Institution, Bureau American Ethnology Bulletin 151:485–507. Washington, D.C.: Government Printing Office.

1984 The Shoshoni-Crow Sun Dance. Norman: University of Oklahoma Press.

Walker, James R.

1917 The Sun Dance and Other Ceremonies of the Oglala Division of the Teton Dakota. American Museum of Natural History, Anthropological Papers 16:50–221.

1980 Lakota Belief and Ritual. Edited by Raymond J. DeMallie and Elaine A. Jahner. Lincoln: University of Nebraska Press.

1982 Lakota Society. Edited by Raymond J. DeMallie. Lincoln: University of Nebraska Press.

1983 Lakota Myth. Edited by Elaine A. Jahner. Lincoln: University of Nebraska Press.

Wallis, Wilson D.

1947 The Canadian Dakota. American Museum of Natural History, Anthropological Papers 41:1–226.

Weinstein, Edwin A.

1962 Cultural Aspects of Delusion: A Study of the Virgin Islands. New York: Press of Glenco.

Wilson, Michael

1981 Sun Dances, Thirst Dances and Medicine Wheels: A Search for Alternative Hypotheses. *In* Megaliths to Medicine Wheels: Boulder Structures in Archeology, pp. 333–70. Proceedings of the 11th

Annual Conference of the Archeology Association of the University of Calgary, Alberta.

Wissler, Clark
1905 Decorative Art of the Sioux Indians. American Museum of Natural History, Bulletin 18:231–75.
1907 Some Protective Designs of the Dakota. American Museum of Natural History, Anthropological Papers 1:21–53.
1912 Societies and Ceremonial Associations in the Oglala Division of the Teton-Dakota. American Museum of Natural History, Anthropological Papers 11:1–99.

Wood, W. Raymond, and Margot Liberty, eds.
1980 Anthropology on the Great Plains. Lincoln: University of Nebraska Press.

Zimmerly, David W.
1969 On Being an Ascetic: Personal Document of a Sioux Medicine Man. Pine Ridge Research Bulletin 10:46–71.

Index